The Three R's

Recruiting, Retaining &
Rewarding Your Volunteer Team

DR. BILL WITTICH

Knowledge Transfer Publishing

Manufactured in the United States of America

ISBN: 1928794068
ISBN: 9781928794066

Knowledge Transfer Publishing
8650 Heritage Hill Drive
Elk Grove, CA 95624

Tel: 916-601-2485
billwittich@comcast.net
www.volunteerpro.com

Knowledge Transfer books may be purchased for educational, business, or sales promotional use. Please write or call for details.

To Ann, my life and business partner, without whose love and support this book would still be in my dreams

CONTENTS

INTRODUCTION...

No matter how big and powerful government gets, and the many services it provides, it can never take the place of volunteers.

Ronald Reagan

The purpose of this book is to help you build a more successful volunteer program. Simply stated, that is it, but simple the task is not. It will require a large dose of common sense, combined with a solid understanding of people, a dab of contemporary management and leadership theory, plus a large amount of praise and recognition. People volunteer for many different reasons and the more we know about our volunteers the easier our recruiting and the higher our retention rate. Getting and keeping good people is really the key to a successful volunteer program.

This book has evolved from many years of working with volunteers. Having worked as a volunteer in many different settings, I was usually well treated and therefore enjoyed my volunteer activities. But every once in a while I felt a little exploited or even ignored by the volunteer organization and found myself losing interest in volunteering. Sometimes, it was simply feeling a lack of appreciation on the part of the director of the volunteer program. Quite often, as a volunteer coordinator, I found myself doing things that caused me to lose volunteers, even though I was unaware of exactly what was causing this to happen. This book will share a number of these situations and hopefully my experiences and stories will give you food for thought.

Corporate America has moved from a psychology of management as controller of people to an aura of leadership allowing employees to develop their own environment. The tools they use to create this setting are empowerment, team building, recognition, praise, and coaching. As

I reviewed these leadership practices, it became clear that much of what was shining in that arena would directly transfer to the volunteer setting. These practices of team building and coaching all apply with little or no change.

This book will alter the paradigm of how we in the non-profit and governmental volunteer settings manage volunteers. Much of this book is simply common-sense, and some of it is restating age old principles of doing the right thing. Hopefully, this book reinforces Nordstrom's one-page employee handbook stating that associates should "use their own best judgement in all things." My thoughts have been influenced by the writings of Ken Blanchard and that little book, *The One-Minute Manager*, which stresses that the best way to develop people is by catching them doing things right and praising them for it.

Truthfully, the job of being a volunteer coordinator is whatever it takes! And what it takes is a person willing to practice many roles, being a social director, a coach, a cheerleader, a task master, a facilitator, an entertainer, a leader and a friend. This book will hopefully convince you that we in the volunteer world tend, at times, to be too serious. Maybe, it's because we work in a helping arena and that we get caught up in the seriousness of this environment. Our volunteers enjoy their work and want to have fun. I suggest that we all look at Southwest Airlines past CEO Herb Kellegher as a model for creating a work environment that is absolutely fun. This theme of lightening up the volunteer place will run through the chapters of this book.

1

NO MORE WARM BODIES!

Be a yardstick of quality. Some people aren't used to an environment where excellence is expected.

Stephen Jobs

Recently, while wandering through a mall, I saw a large poster on the wall. It stated:

Wanted, Volunteers
No Experience Necessary
Warm Bodies Wanted
Just Come On In!

Is this really what you want? Just warm bodies? No experience? Anyone who is interested regardless of their motives? I don't really think so.

The first point is that advertising doesn't really work. In fact, a recent study has shown that only about 9% of all volunteers come from an advertisement. In fact, over 90% of all volunteers come from someone asking them to volunteer.

The real danger of the "warm body" ad is that you might have 100 volunteers show up excited to start! Let's be honest, you post the ad expecting to locate those five to ten volunteers you need. What do you do with those 100 people that responded? You select the first ten and lose the other 90 volunteers. These 90 volunteers that you do not select will be "unhappy campers" and will probably never volunteer for you again, and in fact, will spread negative coments about how you operate. One thing we do know, is that if we ask someone to volunteer, we had better be ready to use their talents. Volunteers have little patience for someone who doesn't use their interest in a reasonable amount of time.

The real issue is that you were really not interested in warm bodies - you were looking for experienced, knowledgeable, talented volunteers to perform specific tasks. In fact, you don't search for volunteers, you search for work that needs to be done. At one point I was working to start a city volunteer program, and to gather enough jobs for volunteers I sent out a letter calling for support from various city departments. My letter to each department manager stated the following, "Do you have any work in your department that volunteers can do?" That was the wrong letter! What came back from these departments was the following. No! We have no work that volunteers are capable of performing. You see the mindset of these department heads? They were afraid of getting a group of warm bodies, untrained and incapable of performing anything, but basic tasks. Even for basic tasks, volunteers require training and supervision, hardly worth the effort. I was confused and even hurt by their lack of support for the new volunteer effort our city was putting together. But after a few cups of coffee, I found out that each manager had a concern about the time and effort required to train the volunteers.

Having realized my naive efforts, I sent another letter requesting any assignments that the departments needed filled and that they might schedule over the next year, if the required resources appeared. Of course, the departments thought I was indicating dollar resources, but I meant highly qualified professional talent who could perform those jobs. For example, one department indicated a need for a web site. I contacted a local university and obtained the services of an outstanding graduate student in engineering who developed the city web site. Not once did the department have any thoughts about the quality of work performed by this computer consultant. The department head said they would like to retain this expert if the consulting budget would allow. They had no idea that I had recruited the services of a student volunteer from the university service-learning program. The difference was clear, It was the attitude of the department head. But the real issue was the way I had approached the departments. I needed to stress the fact that I had a group of fellow professionals willing to assist their program.

My approach since that time has been to assume that every person asked to volunteer is a professional with skills and talent. That is so true, everyone in life has gathered a collection of specific skills and talents that they use as moms and dads and employees. Our job is to search out these talents and put the volunteer to work making use of these talents. The right person, at the right time, with the right talents, is the key to good volunteer results. The key is selecting the right people for the right job.

John Maxwell, in his book, *Developing the Leaders Around You,* quotes Red Auerbach, longtime Boston Celtics president, who says, "How you select people is more important than how you manage them, once they are on the job." If you start with the right people, you won't have problems later on. If you select the wrong people, for whatever reason, you're in serious trouble and all the revolutionary management techniques in the world won't bail you out.

Many leadership gurus suggest that selecting the right players determines 80% of the success of any organization. But equally important to selecting the right people, is having the right expectations for your volunteers. You may have heard about the *Pygmalion Theory.* It says that if we expect someone to succeed, they probably will and if we expect them to fail, they probably will. This theory has a lot to do with the self-fulfilling prophecy idea. That is, when a person predicts that something will happen, they setup an expectation. This expectation actually changes the way the person behaves. Think back to a time in your life when you had someone, your dad or a coach, who believed in you and they pushed you to excel. You did excel. Their support or, more importantly, their expectations about you, created a positive feeling in you that led to improved performance.

James Kouzez and Barry Posner, in their book, *Encouraging the Heart,* share a thought that says, "Simply stated, people must believe that they are capable of solving the problem, of finding a new and better way, or they won't. They can't if they don't believe in themselves, in their own capabilities..." This feeling of self-expectation is key to their success. But more important than the their self-expectation is the support and reinforcement that the volunteer coordinator must give to each volunteer. Since we know that both high expectations and low expectations will influence a volunteer's performance, we must work on the high expectation, since it will cause a positive impact on the individual. This positive impact, according to Kouzez and Posner, will encourage the heart.

2

PEOPLE REALLY DON'T VOLUNTEER!

The most enthusiastic givers in life are the real lovers of life. They experience the soul-joy that comes from responding with the heart rather than the head.

Helen Steiner Rice

Think about it. When you were sitting in a PTA meeting and the leader asked for volunteers to head a busy committee, did everyone say YES? Did anyone say YES? Did you immediately throw up your hand? You always need more information before you decide. In fact, usually, unless someone directly asks us and tells us why they selected us, we don't volunteer.

Ask - that's the critical item. I recently saw an article in the *Los Angeles Times* with the headline "More teens would volunteer if asked, but many just aren't approached." It says that many teens are likely to become community volunteers, only if they're asked. But nobody is asking them. The latest Gallup Poll shows teens are four times more likely to volunteer if asked, than if they are not asked. Since people don't walk in and say, "I want to volunteer," we need to design our training program around two things. First, how to find people to ask and then, that all important training in how to ask.

Where should we be looking for volunteers? It's not so much where to look as it is how to look for volunteers. It's a change in mindset. Think about visiting one of your local stores. Maybe it's the FedEx Office, your local speedy print shop. You walk in and the woman behind the counter says, "Good morning, can I help you?" What about her? Isn't she a potential volunteer for your organization? Of course she is. But how do you convert her from a person helping us in a store to a person helping us as a volunteer? Recruiting volunteers is a three-step process. The steps are prospect, cultivate, and ask (PCA). Prospects are potential volunteers. Where do we find potential volunteers? Well, the answer is everywhere, but your best prospects are those close to you. I call this the ONE SQUARE MILE rule. By this, I mean that the people within your personal one square mile are your most likely volunteers. One square mile is just a way of saying that people like to affiliate with organizations where they already have a connection. This connection might be the school where their children attend. Or it might be the church they attend, or even the city they live in. It makes a lot of common sense for someone to volunteer for an organization that they have an attachment with.

Let's go back to that prospect at your local print shop just down the street. You go in there all the time and know all the sales people in the store. In order words, you already have a relationship with these people. They are within your one square mile rule. Everytime you visit the store and converse with these people, you talk about your needs. Isn't that true? Well, you do talk about your printing needs, correct? But you do not talk about your volunteer needs. These are prospects, potential volunteers, and they might find your organization of interest. It is true that most people do think about giving a little time to a volunteer organization, but most have no direct connection to your non-profit, and without that connection the thought remains just a thought and it never moves to action.

So how do you get this person to consider volunteering for you? Step 2 of the PCA approach, CULTIVATE. Cultivation simply means to inform people of the volunteer opportunities that your organization offers. You need to do it in as exciting a way as you can. Most people looking for volunteers use the old tin cup method, they go begging. Wrong! The best way to attract people to volunteering is to excite them about the opportunities for them when they volunteer with your organization.

Let me give you an example of cultivation. My friend Jefferey was a prime prospect to volunteer for the Friendly Visitors program of which I was a volunteer. One day, following a round of golf, I asked Jefferey if he would consider becoming a volunteer for the group. He said, "Bill, that is so weird!" That surprised me. I said, "Why is that weird, Jefferey?" He said that just this week he had received a brochure on the Friendly Visitor program. I laughed and said, " Yes, you did, I sent it to you!" My point is that before I asked my friend to volunteer I made sure that he had all the information about the program. This is the cultivation we are discussing. Cultivation means nothing more than giving someone all the information about your group that they need to help them decide to volunteer. People do not volunteer for organizations that they know nothing about. People need to be informed as to the needs, and the groups filling those needs. Everyone has only so much time to volunteer, and they will consider whether your group is the most effective use of their time.

Cultivation takes place in many locations. Mine occurred on the golf course, allowing me 18 holes to discuss my volunteer activities at the Friendly Visitors program. Sometimes cultivation might occur at work, or during a car pool ride, or over a cup of morning coffee. My point is that it is a planned activity. Once you locate a prospect, you set out to inform or cultivate this person. You are giving them enough information about your group to help them make an informed decision to join your agency. This is very different than advertising. Advertising assumes that the person will see a poster and jump up and volunteer. The advertisement might be a part of your cultivation program, as it helps to inform your prospect, but it is not a stand-alone recruiting tool. This is the process of marketing, a planned strategy to continually recruit prospects for your organization. There are many marketing tools available, just as there are many different volunteers to recruit.

But all of this cultivation will go to waste if the last step is not applied. That last step of the PCA approach is to ASK. See, we have located a potential volunteer, given them all the information about your organization's needs and how they might fit into your group, and even discussed what's in it for them. But if nobody asks them to volunteer, they will not become a volunteer. People need to have information and time to consider if your group has a fit with their needs. Your printed materials, website and social media need to perform this task in a marketing sense, but they will not do the asking for you. It takes a person to do the ask. Brochures don't recruit volunteers, people do. That person answers questions, explains the process, and at the right moment, asks the person to volunteer.

3

WHY DO PEOPLE SAY YES TO VOLUNTEERING?

*Each citizen should play his part in the community
according to his individual gifts.*

Plato

People volunteer for many reasons, sometimes altruism, sometimes personal, but always for a purpose. We need to understand that purpose in order to attract and retain the volunteer. For many, it's a way of giving back. You will hear volunteers say, "My mother received excellent care in this hospital and I want to repay some of that kindness." Another volunteer will say, "When I was growing up, there was a Boy Scout leader who made a difference in my life, and I want to be one of those who makes a difference to a young boy." The concept of giving back is strong in most volunteers' minds.

Many volunteers will tell you that they want to meet people. They are new to the neighborhood, have been home raising children, or haven't met the kind of people they would like to have as their friends. Do you remember the old days? You would move into a new neighborhood and out came the welcome wagon, neighbors brought over bread and cookies, and you stood talking to these people for hours. Where are these people today? They are probably still there, but like us, they are working two jobs and raising households. Time is the most precious commodity among all of us.

Other people are looking to **learn** new skills. Skills that they can use in the workplace or to enhance their job possibilities. They will ask you about the possibility of working with your agency's computer and e-mail system. Many people, having been home raising the kids, feel out of touch with the technology of today's business world. E-mail, web sites, computer operating systems, networks, these are all a foreign language and they are looking to help and learn at the same time.

Some people are looking for relationships. They are wanting to meet the kind of people that they can share time with. So they can share the same kinds of interests. Many people today are alone and lonely. Where do you make these kinds of close, meaningful relationships with people like you? For some, it's at a gym, for others it's in the workplace, but for many it's the volunteer setting.

Sometimes volunteers are looking for a connection. For example, parent volunteers want to help in their child's classroom because it connects them with the school environment. They hope to gain an insight into the teaching-learning experience that goes on for their children. The parent gets to know the teacher on a first-name basis and feels free to ask about homework assignments and might even learn how to do that new math! For the teacher, the parent volunteers are a wonderful connection with the community outside their classroom. It brings support from the parents and from the business community. It's sometimes easy to forget that these moms and dads are in the local business community. And they have a strong interest in making that classroom prosper.

Some volunteers are there to spy! People sometimes volunteer to gain an insight into an organization. Parents might be curious about what really goes on inside today's schools. Citizens wonder about the functioning of city hall. A volunteer wonders if a career in healthcare might be an option, and volunteers to see how it feels for them. Just as people volunteer to gain workplace experience, people volunteer to assess the environment and see if it fits them for a potential career.

Some volunteers are actually looking for a job! Watch out, it may be yours! Many volunteer coordinators started as volunteers in a place similar to where they now are paid staff members. Other volunteers are career sampling, trying a workplace on for size. Police Explorer Scouts are young people trying to find out if a law enforcement career might be right for them. Many volunteer firefighters are searching for a paid firefighter position, and many fire departments are open about the fact that they get to try out new candidates as volunteers.

Some people are looking for a place where they can use those skills and **talents** that they have developed in the paid workplace. Many people today are frustrated in their paid jobs because they are not given an opportunity to try different things or to make decisions. They are ready to jump into volunteer leadership roles and would find the opportunity to be refreshing. The lack of promotion in their paid job allows them to search for ways to move ahead in the volunteer environment.

Some folks are just looking to have some fun! One of the frustrating things to me is how little lightness and outright fun is to be found at many volunteer places. Remember that many people work all week long without having a good time. This should never happen in the volunteer setting. It is okay, in fact it should be standard, that the volunteer place is a fun environment. Yes, we can really enjoy what we do, even if the work is serious and meaningful.

We have just touched on a few of the hundreds of reasons why people start their volunteer careers. The important thing is to ask the volunteer why they are volunteering. And listen. Be sure to probe a little to get past the standard, "I want to do good" type of response. Every volunteer wants to do good, but what brought this volunteer to your front door? It probably was not altruism, even though that's a part of it for all of us.

4

HIRE THE BEST

You're only as good as the people you hire

Ray Kroc

The single most important thing we do is to select the best volunteers for the job. Picking the best people and placing them in the best assignments that match their skills and interests is the answer to success. Everything is secondary to this one criterion. There is always an assumption that the leader can take anyone and with a little coaching, turn him or her into a winner and the team goes home with the trophy. Isn't what happens to the Little League team down the street? All the local kids apply for the team, some who can play ball and some who can't. Then the coach is told by the parents to play all the kids and is expected to turn out a winning team. We know this is fantasy and it is fantasy to assume that just any one of your members could run the fundraising dinner or deliver meals for your meals-on-wheel program.

This is the equivalent of warm body recruiting, where you simply have a person walk into the club and the next day they are running a community service project. We know that a team in professional sports is only as

good as its players. This is just as true in non-profit management. David
Thielen in his book, *The 12 Simple Secrets of Microsoft Management*, says, "It's
irrelevant what you think the quality of your employees is. What matters
is what the level of quality truly is." This is not to say that the quality of
your volunteers is all that counts, good leaders can still create problems.
Bureaucratic procedures can mess up the flow of work and even cause
members to leave your agency.

Our point here is to come up with a procedure for conducting good
training. The process at Microsoft is worth us considering. They have the
employees in the group hiring for a position train the new hire. If we follow this model we would allow our volunteers in a group to train new volunteers. For example, in your Meals on Wheels unit, the current drivers
would train all new candidates for driver and help make a decision about
those people. The leader would then conduct a separate check- list and
using the members comments and their own reactions to the new member would okay the new drivers. You will find that the current drivers are
concerned about the quality of the new driver and with a little training can
do a good job of making that determination because they are closest to the
job. As an aside, it also builds the self-esteem of the current crew because
you respect them enough to help you make a critical hiring decision.

Selecting the right person is the most critical decision a manager
makes. No matter how desperate you are to fill a position, no matter
what the consequences, do not compromise. Skills are relatively easy to
develop, and knowledge is easy to acquire. But more difficult is changing
someone's attitudes. So, go for people with positive attitudes, personali-
ties that are bright and people who can relate to you and your colleagues.
Experience counts, but, first and foremost, is the desire to succeed.

The late Zig Ziglar, best selling author of *Over The Top*, says that it's
your attitude, not your aptitude, which determines your altitude. This attitude means that you are willing to see the good in things, to see an opportunity when an obstacle faces you, to treat others the way you want to be

treated, to encourage others when they need support, to have something nice to say, and to be willing to maintain your attitude everyday.

Tom Peters says it so well in his book *Reinventing Work*. "Everyone says, 'People are our most important asset.'" In a non-profit, people are our only asset." If you are serious about finding volunteers who will serve your clients, you start with people who are willing to make it happen. Selecting well means being highly selective. One critical skill is your people skills. Chip Bell and Ron Zemke in a light hearted book, *Managing Knock Your Socks Off Service*, talks about staff being good at handling their own emotions, calm under fire, and not susceptible to "catching the stress virus from upset customers."

Your volunteers are truly front-line workers in a customer service sense and they do interact with your customers. These customers are the citizens relating to neighborhood watch volunteers, the patients and family in a hospital setting, and the students in a school classroom. What do the people that your volunteer serves really want? Jeffrey Gitomer in his book, *Customer Satisfaction is Worthless*, says they want "communication, attitude, reliability, and empathy."

Gitomer gives these examples of these four key traits of the person who serves customers:

> *Communication-* "Let me know what I need to know when I need to know it."
> *Attitude-*"Happy, eager, willing, prepared to meet my needs."
> *Reliability-* "Consistent...be there when I need you."
> *Empathy-* "Understand me and my needs. Give me your commitment."

Martin Sandler and Deborah Hudson in their book, *Beyond The Bottom Line*, give an example of nonprofit customer service at the Children's Museum of Indianapolis. "…Kids are the customers, the museum's reason for being; and kids make up the core of the volunteer staff." One volunteer stated that "the training I received, taught me more than how to guide people through the museum, it taught me how to deal with people's concerns, how to explain things clearly and, best of all, how to help make the museum a better place for kids my age."

Every organization has their own process as to how they make the final selection of a new volunteer. But the key is to only bring in volunteers who are willing to meet your organizations mission. Remember to take enough time for your board and volunteers to get to know the prospect before deciding to induct the individual. It is much more difficult to unload the wrong person than having the organization move slowly with its new volunteer decision.

5

MEMBERSHIP IS CRITICAL

This club is for members only.
But once you join,
membership lasts for an eternity.

Ellen Schreiber

Just how much of an impact has the current economy had on non-profits and associations in general? We know that between 1946 and 2000 most volunteer organizations did very well in both membership and retention. The active support of Boomers, the largest generation in history helps non-profits to thrive. But starting in 2000, the bubble burst. Hiring freezes, layoffs and consolidations created a concern among workers in many industries. In 2008, the current recession started across North America. This recession with its unemployment, home foreclosures, inflation and rising gas prices took effect and agencies felt this pinch. It certainly takes money to continue to belong to volunteer. We ask our volunteers for more work, more foundation giving, and attendance at various events, both fundraising, service and social events.

A big retirement wave also started in 2011 as many Boomers reached retirement age and looked at a great opportunity to hit the road in their RVs and trailers. Every day for the next 20 years, about 10,000 per day will cross that retirement threshold according to the Pew Research Center. By 2030, when all baby boomers will have turned 65, about 18 percent of the nation's population will be at least 65 or older compared with about 13 percent now. On the one hand retirement might mean more time for volunteer service, but this time might create a problem itself. It is the desire upon retirement to get away, at least for a while, and the fact that many volunteers are open to extended travel might limit their time to volunteer.

We are facing a crisis if a number of these volunteers decide to leave their volunteering upon retirement. It might create a shift in human capital since much of the leadership in agencies is Boomer-based today. Not only the leadership, but the majority of active volunteers are Boomers. Remember that only a small percentage of volunteers are under the age of forty and joining a non-profit does not tend to top the younger generation's list of things to do.

Many younger prospects will be asking if volunteering has a good return on investment for them. In a study by The William E. Smith Institute For Association Research titled *Generations and the Future of Association Participation* it is pointed out that younger people seek and demand a return for membership investment. These include tangible member services, high levels of accountability to volunteers, identifiable career advantages from volunteering, a sense of professional community, and opportunities to serve within agencies. The authors state that "what we need to know is the right scale and combination of services to meet the desires of younger members." Looking at the sense of professional community and the fact that the largest number of current volunteers are in retirement creates an issue. If the younger members want to rub shoulders with working professionals but the volunteers are no longer working, is that a concern to those younger volunteers?

Maybe the following is good news for agencies. Further research from Generations and the Future of Association Participation illustrates that these younger professionals show a higher willingness than previous generations to join associations. The question is whether this indicates that they are willing to join a professional association or join a non-profit. In the past the professional joined both their professional association and a non-profit organization.

We keep hearing that the 20-30-40-year old professionals simply aren't joiners. Most people feel that as the Boomers retire, participation and membership in most service clubs will begin to fall, unless they can find new ways to engage younger members. This assumption came in part from Robert D. Putnam's *Bowling Alone: The Collapse and Revival of American Community* which said clearly that " Americans were less likely to join voluntary organizations." Putnam gives us his reasons for this trend in non-profit volunteering. He says it included "increasing cynicism about the motives of people in power, higher levels of female workforce participation, population rootlessness among young people, family breakdown, and technologies that made it less and less necessary to interact with others face-to-face."

It might be that Putnam is wrong with his thesis in at least two areas. First, he states that the higher female workforce participation might lower the involvement in volunteering. I find it just the opposite as professional women are finding value in connecting and networking as a way to improve their corporate positions. Secondly, the new technologies will make it easier for agencies to locate individuals that have an interest in networking and service opportunities.

Interesting research comes from the Leigh Bureau which tells us that "younger workers are beginning to show great promise in joining associations, and their future involvement looks better still." One thing we are finding out about this younger generation comes from the Domain

Group, a for-profit marketing group specializing in fundraising services for major charities, is that that they require more return on their charitable investments. They want to know the result of the money and time that they donate to a charity. Based on data based research, the firm tells its nonprofit clients that "a younger donor puts more demands on the organization they support, they want more information and involvement." This indicates that this younger generation will be less check writers and more hands-on volunteers. It also shows us that the younger member will demand a clear statement of results from their local agency. It appears that there is a direct connection between which service clubs are most attractive to younger prospects based on what kind of benefit they might receive when they donate time and money.

One of the keys to membership recruiting and retention will be the amount of connection we make with all our volunteers, but in particular, those younger members

6

WHO VOLUNTEERS MORE,
MEN OR WOMEN?

*A human being is happiest and most successful when dedicated to a
cause outside his own individual, selfish satisfaction.*

Benjamin Spock

Men or women. Who volunteers at a higher rate? Well, in the past, volunteering was a feminine activity. Think about it. Most volunteering was
done by Mom. She volunteered in the hospital gift shop, the school, the
church, or the Red Cross. Men went to work and the women took care of
the kids and volunteered. That was true at least until this past decade. It
was a 15 percent male and 85 percent female volunteering world. Few men
volunteered; most simply saw themselves as the breadwinner and stayed
out of the volunteer place.

But recently, and the most recent Independent Sector Gallup Poll
shows it, men are going into volunteering in large numbers. The question
to consider is why the change? What woke men up to the value of volunteering? When I ask this question in my seminars, I get a wide range of

possible reasons for the spurt in male volunteering. To get away from the wife, to meet ladies, because gender roles are changing, men are feeling guilty about the wife's work load and want to share, men are finally waking up and giving back. I guess each of these might have some truth in them, but, these are not the key reasons.

I usually suggest something that may be startling. Men and women are different! How silly this sounds. But give it a moment's thought. When my wife and I are shopping and I go with her to a craft shop, I am usually bored. And when she comes with me to an electronic toy store, like The Apple Store, I know she is bored. We have different interests, and for much of the time it breaks down along gender lines. Men usually don't have interest in the traditionally female volunteer roles. We guys just don't care for the candy striper jobs or the hospital gift store positions. So what has caused the movement of men into volunteering? Something has, because the most recent Gallup Poll shows that 45 percent of men are now volunteering. It is interesting to note that the percentage of women volunteering hasn't changed over the last few decades. Historically, about half of all women in America have always volunteered. The number of women continues to hold steady and in the newest survey, 52 percent of women volunteer.

Let's think about this rapid increase in the number of men volunteering. It has a lot to do with the new areas of volunteer activity. One of the keys to this male growth is Habitat for Humanity. Not so much Habitat, but the kind of volunteer assignments required by Habitat. Think about the guys in hard hats, carrying hammers to a construction site. Men enjoyed the work. Men will volunteer if the work assignments interest them. Then along came governmental volunteering. City hall and the police departments began volunteer programs. Neighborhood watch, community policing, Citizens on Patrol, RSVP citizen patrol. Parks and Recreation, nature activities, and athletics in general sparked male interests.

The most interesting thing about all this new male activity, which was led by a change in the volunteer positions, is that women have also shown an interest in these positions. Today, women represent a large number of the volunteers in Habitat for Humanity and the sheriff's department. Women found a new opportunity for volunteering in those areas. But sometimes this movement of women into what the men considered their private volunteering domain came with problems. Not always were women welcomed with open arms at the local volunteer fire department or at the emergency rescue service. But the good news is that most of that resentment by men has passed and we are seeing an almost equal number of women in those public service volunteer programs.

When you look at the amount of time given, both sexes contribute about the same. Both men and women contribute about 4.2 hours per week. So, when you think about gender equality, we are just about there in the volunteer world, men and women volunteer at nearly the same rate (45 percent men vs 52 percent women).

7

DEMAND EXCELLENCE

The leader finds the dream
and then the people.
The people find the leader
and then the dream.

John Maxwell

Somehow people think of volunteers as people who care, but really can't get the job done. The whole concept that we hear so often that they are "only volunteers" says it all. Even members have been heard saying that they are only volunteers, therefore don't expect too much of them. Or the attitude that the volunteer is not getting paid, so don't expect a professional attitude or performance. This is absolutely silly. Look at college sports players, they don't get paid, but they will play their hearts out on the football field or basketball court. Why doesn't the college player say, "Well I am just a college player, don't expect too much from me until I get a big salary in the pros." You and I know that this attitude would never get them to the professional ranks. Also the fans don't pay high dollars for college stadium fifty-yard seats and then say, don't expect too much

THE THREE R'S 25

because they are only beginners. So why do we allow this minimal expectation from our volunteers? It's our job to raise the bar and begin to expect excellence, to commit to excellence.

Lou Holtz, in his book, *Winning Every Day*, gives it to us directly when he says, " Leaders must challenge and inspire. I know that many people today believe that demanding excellence is politically incorrect. We are supposed to accept whatever an individual gives us as the natural expression of his ability and not pressure him or her by asking for anything more. Nonsense." Our job as leaders is just like the college coach, that is, to find and develop the best volunteers we can. Our job is to encourage our players and help them reach their goals. Every volunteer arrives at your front door fired up to perform a job that will make a difference. They have a burning desire to create change for people.

Your volunteer's join to do service that will make a difference. So what happens? Many times it is the lack of leadership on the part of the leader and the board that deflates that excitement. Lou Holtz uses the example of General Patton who when quizzed about the ability of his army to finish one battle, march one hundred miles and then fight another encounter in less than forty-eight hours, said "That's what we're in business for." Every volunteer also thinks that way. These high standards start with us. We must know and understand what we are there to do. We have a job to perform that makes a difference in people's lives. We use volunteers to accomplish this task. We could not get it done without them.

Our volunteers must be continually motivated to continue their daily chase toward getting the work done. That's when we must put on our coach's cap and start to work. The leader must have the traits of leadership and be the kind of person that people want to follow. I have seen many definitions that try to explain the difference between management and leadership, but the best I think comes from Warren Bennis. Warren served as a professor in the Leadership Institute at USC. He said that "managers do things right, but leaders do the right things." When you work in service, doing the right thing is critical. This involves selecting the right people, continually motivating them, and assigning them to the right tasks

8

UNDERSTANDING GENERATIONS

"Different Strokes for Different Folks"

American Idiom

Many volunteers are aging and we are aware that we have a generation of young people that we hope to attract to volunteering. But first, we need to understand how we can best accomplish this. We even need to understand what we mean by generations.

A generation is a group of people based on their age that share a chronological place in history and share experiences that go with it. These experiences give them-shared beliefs and behaviors. Older volunteers have shared beliefs concerning agency traditions and practices. It may be those traditions and practices that create separation from your younger members.

As our more senior volunteers grow older, we need to attract that next generation into volunteering. The natural audience is either the younger generation or baby boomers. Why not both?

Boomers are that group looking toward retirement and they are strong in numbers, over 78 million in the United States alone. They can expect to live to an average age of 83. **That** means their life expectancy is about 8 years longer than our current senior members and this life expectancy is likely to increase during our boomers lifetimes. We may be thinking that all we need to do is recruit more boomers and all our membership problems will go away.

The trouble with that thought is that even these new boomer volunteers are growing older and we will continue to face the same issue of a non-profit full of older volunteers. We also need to be aware that engaging members of different ages is even more critical as younger people enter the workforce. We are going to discuss the two youngest generations, Generation X (born between 1965 and 1980) and millennial (born 1981 to 2001) since that is the group we are looking to attract.

This millennial generation is the largest generation to date and represents the critical future of volunteering. But neither the Gen X nor millennial are entering agencies fast enough to replace our older volunteers who are leaving. Agencies that successfully attract multi-generational members will be the agencies that succeed in the long term. It will be the wise agency that spends time beginning to understand the differences between generations and there are many differences.

Spending time understanding differences will help to avoid tensions between generations. Your younger volunteers may try to jump in feet first, but may not want to do things the way they've always been done. If your agency is being driven by volunteers older than 50 years old, then what can we do to attract those younger ones?

Netanya Stutz, senior marketing manager of the Washington, D.C. based American Hotel & Lodging Association tells us that it's important for us to understand what the younger person's needs are and what they want out of a volunteer organization.

Our younger volunteers want to make a difference in the world, be heard, and feel like they are contributing. We know they live in a fast world, moving at a fast pace and they wonder why everyone is not moving like they are. While our senior volunteers talk about their latest cruise, these younger members are talking career and family issues. There is a disconnect between generations and it should not be occurring in the non-profit.

Part of this disconnect is easy to solve. You did it when you changed from a print newsletter to a digital one. You are doing it by changing from a social hour at the local pub to a family-night activity at the local pizza house. You do it by changing from projects relating to the local senior center to working at a crisis center for moms.

The biggest difference between younger volunteers and more mature ones is what they expect to derive from their volunteering.

Generation X expert Rebecca Ryan captures the Xers skeptical attitude in *Sticking Points* by Haydn Shaw. She sees Gen Xers as " a generation of Americans who have little faith in institutions. In other words, Gen Xers are skeptical. They have a difficult time trusting others, they are obsessively self-reliant, and they don't see themselves as joiners of traditional organizations."

Gen Xers are skeptical of all organizations.

They will attend meetings only if they find them relevant, but they aren't as interested in membership and don't join committees as enthusiastically as Boomers did. It is abundantly clear that young people don't join just to be members. "They don't discharge social capital responsibility by writing a check and being a member of something. That's characteristic of a past generation." according to Arthur Brooks, PhD, director of the Nonprofit Studies Program at the Maxwell School of Citizenship and Public Affairs at Syracuse University.

Younger volunteers tend to leave the volunteer setting faster than your older volunteers. Younger volunteer turnover might be high for a number of reasons. They move fast and want to be challenged. Young people want to feel like they are making an impact. Give young members responsibilities. Listen to their ideas. Most importantly, make them the leaders and let them change things. If they become bored with volunteering, they're gone.

Millennials tend to be loyal to people more than organizations. It is important to get them connected in a hurry when they start volunteering in order to keep them around.

The younger volunteer generations are the Millennials, between 18 and 30 years old and Generation X between 31 and 45 years old. Both of these generations are the young members you are looking to add to your volunteer roster.

Millennials are the first generation carried around in huge SUVs with "baby on board" signs in the back window. These are the children of the large "Baby Boomer generation." They are the first group who received a trophy whether they were a winner or not because every child deserved a trophy or you might damage their self-esteem. Sometimes referred to as Generation Y, this group prefers to be called the millennial generation. They are larger than the boomer generation; in fact, they make up nearly a third of the U.S. population. This is the largest generation of young people since the 1960s. They seem to text more than they talk. They text rather than e-mail. They are connected to dozens of social networks and communicate with people all over the globe. They have never been without computers or smart phones. They're well educated, skilled in technology and very self-confident.

To Gen X and Y, formal volunteering may seem time-consuming, not very productive, and limited in structure. They just don't seem to fit their lifestyles. Lisa Johnson in *Mind Your Xs and Ys* tells us, "They can lack immediacy, fun, and a true sense of impact." In many ways it might mean that they are not waiting to fit in but want to find an organization where they fit better. They are the connected generation that checks Google's websites before applying for college, employment and again, before joining a volunteer setting.

They will likely shop for a volunteer opportunity before joining, and will make their decision based on what they see on their iPhone screen. If the agency does not have a current and active Facebook page and a Twitter account sending Tweets regularly, they will likely never show up to volunteer. When they do show up they will bring a new style and a new perspective. And unless your agency is willing to adapt, they will find them going out the door almost as fast as they enter.

For one thing this generation is going to show up and expect to have a voice. As Lynne Lancaster in her book, *the M-factor* tells us " Millennial are pushing for new forms of leadership and decision-making based on collaboration." They have skills already developed for cooperation, but we wonder how the older volunteers will accept this new way of relating.

The Millennial will certainly challenge the ways many of us run our agencies. For example, Boomers will often do what the Millennial call the "death march" where each person reports on his or her work while everyone listens, or pretends to listen. Millennial wonder why these reports can't be shortened and e-mailed to all of us. Millennial are always asking, "How do we get those older volunteers to listen to us? They don't seem to take us seriously."

Millennial are a highly educated group, three quarters are educated beyond high school and over 25% hold college degrees. Another 25% are currently attending college. They are the most racially and ethnically diverse generation ever in America. Millennial are very concerned about social and environmental issues and are very active in community service. Now let's look at those older young volunteers, Gen Xers.

Generation X, grew up in a very different world than previous generations. Divorce and working moms created "latchkey" kids out of many of these young people. This led to traits of independence, resilience and adaptability.

Generation X feels strongly that they don't want to be micro-managed. At the same time, this generation expects immediate and ongoing feedback, and is equally comfortable giving feedback to others including those on your board. They work well in multicultural settings, desire fun in the agency and expect to be involved in all decisions.

Generation X saw their parents get laid off or face job insecurity. Many of them also entered the workforce when the economy was in a downturn. Because of these factors, they've redefined loyalty. This will be reflected in their volunteering. For example, a Baby Boomer may talk about his dissatisfaction with the agency, but figures it's just a part of volunteering. A Gen Xer doesn't waste time complaining, she starts shopping for another agency to volunteer at. She will first visit online and then by going in the organizations front door.

Gen Xers may also challenge agencies to rethink their structure as they may not have as much time to commit to volunteering as older retired volunteers. Rather than your viewing this as a lack of commitment or interest, this may be an opportunity to think of new ways to engage the younger volunteer. Soon to be over mid 40s, they are resourceful and hardworking.

They work well in multicultural settings. Tamara Erickson in her book *What's Next Gen X?* tells us "Xers became the first generation of youth to develop a global perspective and empathy, often through the televised events that raised funds for and awareness about AIDS, apartheid, world famine and a host of other global issues."

9

STOP RECRUITING / START ATTRACTING

*In many ways, when you're young and sexy, it's very annoying
to be whistled at and to have someone always trying
to attract your attention, but now when it happens
I find myself registering the fact almost warmly.*

Greta Scacchi

Membership is critical for all volunteer agencies. It is critical to continue to add new volunteers, because each year volunteers will leave for a variety of reasons. They move away, they pass away, they lose their interest, and they run out of money, they disagree with the way the agency is going. It does not really matter why they leave, it is important to find new people to replace those who leave. Too many agencies spend months thinking about how to recruit new volunteers. It is more important to find out how to attract volunteers into your agency.

If your agency is not attractive to a number of people in your community, you might as well stop searching for volunteers. Attraction must come first. This is a major change for agencies to move from an older view of recruitment to a new area of building attraction. Wikipedia tells us that attraction means the drawing of one object towards another.

The question we need to deal with is how we entice guests to visit our agency and not only come back but convert them into committed and dedicated volunteers. We need to decide exactly who we want to attract and why. We know that we need to be engaging, and if we engage our guests will it help them to decide to join. Maybe Seth Godin has it right in his book *Tribes* when he says that a tribe is a group of people connected to one another, connected to a leader, and connected to an idea. Godin says that "Tribes need leadership, they need connection and growth and something new." They need change. His major theme in the book rings with me. That is "You can't have a tribe without a leader and you can't be a leader without a tribe." Is he talking about your volunteer tribe? I think so. Where is a strong volunteer program without a strong leader? And where is a strong leader without a strong agency?

We are not asking just anyone to volunteer. We're looking to attract busy, successful, motivated people who care. The key thought is that we are not looking to recruit warm bodies; we are looking to attract the right people. Attracting the right people means you must put together a program that will help to locate these people. In the corporate world, we call that marketing. In the volunteer world, we call that Public image.

You have to build your marketing first before anyone even knows you exist. Marketing is a tool used to build attraction in your program. Public image allows people to see what the your agency offers even before they see themselves in it. Marketing in the past meant putting articles in your local newspaper. Today it means using various forms of social media to gain the eyes of those prospective volunteers.

Your audience needs to know that you are in their community. Prospective members either live or work in your community and in either case they need to know that you are there. It is true that you need to invite people to visit your agency, but unless they are aware of all the good things your volunteers do, it will be more difficult to arrange that visit.

Today many agencies are having a hard time attracting volunteers into its fold. Their volunteers numbers have not increased over the past year with the exception that they may have lost a few. This chapter will explore how agencies can be successful in growing its volunteer membership. I think most of us will agree that if our program is to remain strong then we must continue to add new volunteers.

These new volunteers must include a mix of younger, middle aged and older members. It must include gender and ethnic diversity as well. It is this diversity that increases the quality of an agencies membership.

Mark Levin in *Millennium Membership* says it so well, "It's not your father's (or Mother's) organization anymore." He explains that only the agencies that understand the value of adding diversity will succeed in attracting members of any age. This means that you may need to change your recruiting process. It is critical for all leaders to understand that what brought them into volunteering may not be the same thing that will bring this in the next generation of volunteers. It may not even be the idea of change; it may be the speed of this change.

We will discuss these changes and offer suggestions for helping agencies adjust and understand what it will take to find new volunteers. We must think about change, not only the changes in the organization, but the changes occurring today in the lives of our volunteers. We must be aware that technology is changing everything about the non-profit world.

Many volunteer meetings are held these days through *Go-To-Meeting*, where we all connect our computers. This saves time and allows us to stay off the road allowing our busy volunteers more time for work and family. My point is that technology has already changed much about volunteering.

The goal is to understand what volunteers expect and how to offer it to them. It is critical to understand your prospective volunteers's views, if we are to attract them into your program. We need to see what is going on in their lives, both their personal, family and volunteer lives. By understanding all three parts, it will help us to see how it affects their view of volunteering for you.

Your club needs to invest in technology and use it to attract new volunteers. Technology such as websites, blogs, Facebook and Twitter are no longer an option, they are a given. Non-profits must be at the forefront of social media to attract new volunteers, particularly those younger ones. Just take a look around Starbucks and watch those young professionals interacting with their smart phones, tablets and computers. These tools are their networking lives.

The fresh perspective and out-of-the-box thinking that younger volunteers can bring may open new avenues for your agency. Through this, younger members may be able to bring a new network of younger volunteers that will be the future for carrying out your mission. While young people can often be counted on to know what is new and hot in the technology world, they can bring more to the table than just being able to set up the LCD projector with ease. Many young people are enthusiastic fundraisers, marketing whizzes, financial geniuses, and special-events gurus.

While the current excitement is finding young people to bring in, there may well be another group of prospects that we might focus on. Those are that large group of retiring Boomers that could help to increase our volunteer base. They are a vital group of healthy, wealthy and wise potential volunteers that we may overlook if we are not aware of them. They are very different from those young prospects in many ways and the attraction process is different for both groups.

You may wonder why we are not looking at those in-between ages, those prospects between the ages of 40 and 65. We certainly are interested in bringing them on board, but in many cases they are already our volunteers and are leading our organization today.

But we hope that this book will convince you that all generations are needed for you to continue your volunteer drive to the future. It is just that the focus will be on these two primary areas of focus, the younger ones and those Baby Boomers, and hopefully you will agree with the value of your focus on these two generations. One thing that both the younger and the Boomer generations have is endless energy.

This is energy that they are looking to throw into a cause that they care about, or that will further their professional careers or retirement days. Incorporating both generations into your group can add this much needed shot of energy and foster new, different, and progressive ideas that can reenergize the agency. If you expect the best from a young member, you will get it. If you expect that the new Boomer members will give their all, you are right. I believe all of us are in agreement that we need to attract new volunteers into our agency.

10

RECRUITING...THE MAGIC WAY!

It is not fair to ask others to do what you are not willing to do yourself.

Eleanor Roosevelt

The next question relates to the best way to recruit volunteers and who, in your organization, should do the recruiting. Well, it's not the volunteer coordinator! The best recruiters are your enthusiastic, satisfied volunteers. Let me share with you the "magic way" to recruit. Every volunteer recruits <u>one</u> volunteer as good as they are! Think about that. You are giving the responsibility to each volunteer to find <u>one volunteer,</u> and not just one, but one as good as the volunteer doing the asking. The number one is critical, for, if you ask your volunteer to find five volunteers, it's overwhelming and frightening.

Let me tell you a story about one of my best volunteers. Her name is Laura. I said, "Laura, aren't you in a carpool with 4 other ladies? Have you ever talked with them about your volunteer activities?" Knowing volunteers' enthusiasm, I bet she talked all the time about her volunteer activity. I then said, "Laura, have you ever asked any of these ladies to volunteer?" Laura looked perplexed, and said,

"Huh?... never thought about that." It's not that she didn't think about asking, it's that she really didn't want to ask. Why not? It has a lot to do with the fear of rejection that most salespeople fear. Why are they afraid to ask for an order, or for money, or to be a volunteer? You know why, it's that old fear of failure, of having someone say "no" to you. It's bad enough when someone says no, and you don't know them, but can you imagine how you would feel if your best friend says no? It does feel like failure. So how can we make it Okay to ask? How can we remove that feeling of failure? We need to praise the ask, and not concern ourselves with the yes or no that the volunteer hears.

Let me tell you how that has worked at one agency where the volunteers were fundraising ... they had ten volunteers, each one was asked to raise a thousand dollar gift. They were all given the names of qualified prospects, and out they went to do the critical ask. When each volunteer returned, he/she was asked if he/she completed the ask. Each volunteer said yes, that they had contacted their prospect and they did "ask." As each volunteer said yes, they did ask their prospect, the coordinator went to the bulletin board and put a large gold star next to that volunteer's name on the list. After she did this about three times, the volunteers all yelled, "Stop!",

"You didn't even bother to ask the important question, did I get the money?" She said "No, I didn't ask that question and it's not really an important question." You see, when you are raising money, or when you are raising friends, the important thing is for your volunteers to ASK. No ask, no gifts or no new volunteers. Isn't that true? Both fundraising and friendraising involve a numbers game! Both require a number of people asking to get to the very important YES. If enough people are asked, the volunteers will raise the money and will recruit those volunteers. Our praise to our volunteers must be for the fact that they asked, not because they raised money or recruited volunteers, but because they had the courage to ask.

There is no difference between fundraising and friendraising. They both require the ask and everybody faces the fear of asking and the fear of rejection. So take the monkey off your back concerning volunteer recruiting. It does feel good to give that responsibility to the people it belongs to, your volunteers. When you transfer the responsibility of recruiting to your volunteers, you will need to assume another responsibility. The responsibility is the training of your volunteers in sales, or more specifically, in how to ask.

11

NO BAD APPLES...

It isn't the people you fire who make your life miserable,
it's the people you don't.

Harvey MacKay

I believe in the Marine Corps philosophy of volunteer recruiting. You know, they are always looking for a few good men & women. Aren't you also? They talk about the "few, the proud", aren't we also looking for a few quality volunteers? And we are looking for <u>good</u> volunteers. We do not want any bad apples in our volunteer basket. How do we keep those bad apples out of our basket? It's called screening. We develop a process of screening that follows a general rule that goes like this, the level of screening depends on the level of risk.

If the risk of the volunteer causing a problem is low, the amount of time and money spent on screening is equally low. If you are recruiting people to help clean up your downtown city park next Saturday morning, the chance of someone causing your organization much concern is low. A person raking leaves or picking up trash will not be a high risk. True, they might injure themselves or another volunteer by accident, but still, the true risk is low, therefore the level of screening should be low. But if your volunteer is to be left alone with children or vulnerable adults, the risk is very high and your screening process must be more involved.

Screening begins during the recruiting process. As you talk to prospects about the opportunities for them as volunteers, you are making decisions about the likelihood of that person serving as a volunteer. In particular, when a prospect drops in and asks to volunteer, you are very much aware of your feelings about that person. Yes, I am suggesting that you should trust your feelings about each potential volunteer. You interview a lot of people and you do have good perceptions about people. Have you ever interviewed a "weird person?" Remember your feelings? You were sitting across the desk from a person, thinking to yourself, I don't feel okay about this person, but I don't have any reason to turn this person down. My advice to everyone at this point is to turn the person down. You have no problem legally with this situation because you are dealing with volunteers, not paid employees. It's your decision, not the potential volunteers.

Screening continues with having the person fill out an application. Your application asks for three references, one personal, one employment and one volunteer. Each reference requests the name and phone number of the reference as well as the way that the reference knows the person.

One important consideration is that if you ask someone for references, you must check those references. Your other volunteers put faith in the fact that you check references and that they are working with folks who have been checked.

Sometimes volunteer directors assume that the act of asking for references helps to screen out bad apples. They think that people who might have background problems will not give references, sort of a self-screening device. But the reality is that even your bad apples will give references, maybe assuming that you don't really plan to check them.

I always check references on the phone, never by mail. I want to hear the tone of voice and listen for any hesitation that the reference might express. Remember that you are really checking for red flags. Red flags are those things that make you worry about the individual being checked. These red flags include the reference being unwilling to give you details about a person's background, or even a person taking a long time in responding to your question. Sometimes it's what the person doesn't say that makes you nervous. Often they give a partial response or tend to avoid a direct question concerning the person.

Three references are a minimum. The first reference to check is the one the person has given to you as a personal reference. You realize that this is normally a friend of the potential volunteer. You may wonder of what value this is assuming friends will not say negative things about a friend. You would be amazed at what friends will say about each other! It also depends on how you ask the questions. Ask the question in this way, "John Mulligan has applied as a volunteer with XYZ Agency and has given us your name as a personal reference." That's it, say no more, and wait. The longer it takes the person to respond the more likely you have a red flag. This person might be trying to figure out how to state something positive but avoid any negative items. Be careful to avoid leading the question by stating that "John told us that he and you have been best friends since high school," as it might lead to a very different response. The person might say, "That's right, we are old friends." People might cover for each other as friends.

When you call for an employment check, do not expect much information. Companies will verify only that the person has worked there or continues to be employed by them. They will also give you the dates of employment, but that is generally all the information you will receive. But, this is of some help. Suppose you find out that the person has never been employed by that firm? That would worry me. I do not trust people who lie, I wonder why they are being dishonest. Reference checking is looking for any red flags in order to make a decision to bring that volunteer aboard.

The best person to ask about a potential volunteer's background is another volunteer coordinator. They are like you. They know people. If someone has volunteered somewhere before, that is the best place to ask about their performance. Most people who apply to volunteer have been volunteers in the past. When you call another coordinator it is like talking to yourself, they will be honest about that person's background. I follow this series of questions. It involves three questions every time. First, I ask if they have had an experience with the individual. It might go like this: "Hi Mildred, I have John Mulligan applying to volunteer with us and he has given us your name as a reference." If she says "Yes," then I worry. If you get a call like this yourself, you will normally say something very enthusiastically such as, "Oh wow, he was one of my best volunteers, send him back to me!" But, when a coordinator doesn't say anything, I worry. This is a red flag. Then I ask question two, "You are not saying much about this past volunteer, want to say more?" If they then say "No, I don't want to say more than to acknowledge that they did volunteer here," then I worry more. Red flag number two. I then ask question three, "Would you allow John Mulligan to come back and volunteer at your place again?" If the volunteer coordinator says no, I would then follow my three strikes, you're out, formula!

12

KNOW YOUR PLAYERS!

*I will have no man work for me who has not the capacity
to become a partner.*

J.C. Penney

Coach Rick Pitino is well known by all basketball fans. Coach Pitino led the Kentucky Wildcats to a spectacular National Championship, and is currently the coach of the University of Louisville. In his book, *Success Is A Choice*, he discusses just how important it is to really know your players. His point is that for a team to be successful, not only does the coach need to understand each player, but the team members need to understand each other. John Wooden, another outstanding basketball coach, this time from UCLA, states that for a coach to be successful, he must do two things. First, appreciate your players for who they are, and second, believe they will do their best.

Both Pitino and Wooden have good advice for volunteer coordinators. We must know everything about each of our volunteers. The more we know about the volunteer, the better we can motivate, reward, and find the best work assignments for him/her. One problem in today's workplace is that people do not feel connected with either management or fellow workers. Companies do not consider it necessary to know about their employees' personal life. Everyone has both a personal and a work place life, and these are not completely separate. Better companies realize that the family members and spouse of an employee must be involved in the everyday activities of a company.

It is our job, starting with our first meeting with a potential volunteer, to gather personal information about the volunteer. I like to sit down informally with a new volunteer and ask them questions about his/her family, employment, and other interests. My application form asks the name, address, phone numbers, and references for checking the volunteer's background. But the most important information gathered at this initial interview is the personal information.

Your success with volunteers does depend upon how well you know them. Knowing more than just the name of the volunteers, knowing their interests, hobbies, and abilities. I use the initial interview to begin gathering background on my volunteers. Questions like, "When is your birthday, your spouse's name, your wedding anniversary, what do you collect, what do you like to do on vacation?" All kinds of personal questions to help me get to know my volunteers.

These questions will be used to allow me to have meaningful conversations, introduce my volunteers around the agency and recognize them in a more personal way. We do not spend enough time getting to know our people, particularly in the work place. Many people at work do not feel connected to others. We must do better than that in the volunteer place. Our task is to work to connect with our volunteers.

During this first meeting with a new volunteer, I will gather more information than at any later date. When people are ready to volunteer, they will tell you everything. Just have a conversation and ask questions and jot down their responses. All this information needs to be recorded on their application form and this way it's available as needed. Be sure to hold this first meeting in an informal setting, outside of your office. I like to sit down with them over a cup of Starbucks and just talk in a friendly manner that lets both of us share personal thoughts.

One of the most important things we must do is to get to know our volunteers on a personal level. They give so much of themselves to us, they deserve to be treated like our friends. The more we find out about our volunteers, the more possibilities we have to use personal references in everyday conversation. The opportunity to ask the volunteer about his or her children, about their vacation plans, or that backyard landscaping project, helps the volunteer to feel that we consider them more that just a helper in the shop.

13

DON'T LOOK FOR VOLUNTEERS!

*As a rule...he who has the most
information will have the greatest
success in life.*

Disraeli

It may sound strange in a book that speaks about finding volunteers to start a chapter with "don't look for volunteers." But I really don't look for volunteers, I look for work that needs to done. That is, I search for the work assignments that need to be done. I ask my staff about their needs and what kinds of skills and knowledge it will take to do this job. We do a task analysis for the volunteer position and then we search for the person with these skills.

So, I look for what kinds of work needs to be done around the organization, and then I set out to locate the best person to fill the job. I start by first doing the task analysis, what work needs to be done. Then we discuss what skills, knowledge and attitude it will take for a person to work successfully. After we write this down on our assignment form, we start thinking about the people with the abilities to do the job. When we interview new volunteers, we ask and probe them to find out both what they can do and what they want to do. You have to base your decision to employ the volunteer based on both considerations, what can they do and what do they want to do. If you miss either one, you might have a potential problem. Many times, I have interviewed volunteers who are so excited to start, they say that they will take on any job, even if they lack the needed skills. Or sometimes, I find out they have certain skills and didn't bother to ask if they would enjoy that task. Either way, the volunteer's interest doesn't last because the job is a poor fit for them. Once we complete the task analysis and decide what types of skills we need, how do we get volunteers to say yes to our request? The concept I use is Alpha & Omega... *the beginning and the end.* At the beginning of your career as a professional the most important thing you need is experience. At the other end of your professional career, you are looking for variety. You are also starting to think about retirement and giving back to society. In fact, at the latter part of one's career, there might even be the need to try something very different to relieve the boredom that sometimes sets in. So we have opportunities to gather professional help at both extremes of life, at the beginning, when the person needs experience, but is full of excitement and passion, and at the end of one's career, when they also have the need for a change of scenery.

The best way to gather that experience or get that change of scenery is using a volunteer opportunity. When you are just starting out in your profession, it is difficult to find a position that will allow you to start right in doing it. You are young, inexperienced, having to start at the bottom of the ladder. You might be a college graduate but your first position is always on the bottom rung of the ladder. So why not volunteer for an organization that needs your skills and doesn't worry that you haven't had much experience yet. They need your training. See, at the beginning of your career you need them and they need you. What a perfect exchange; you get that needed experience, they get the results of all your training. Think about the young professor at the university. She was hired because she has a doctorate from an outstanding university, and yet she has no real experience in her field. In fact, the dean that hired her told her just that; "I love your degree, but you have to get some real world background." The non-profit agency is just the place for her to try out those theories she studied in graduate school. Put yourself in the seat of the volunteer coordinator at an agency that needs that young professor's skills. How do you get her signed on to your organization? How do you get that seasoned professional with years of experience and a high fee for that knowledge?

Before we get to that, let's look at how we locate those professionals whose experience we need. Let's say that after a session focused on needs, our organization realizes we need someone to volunteer with an accounting background. We just have to have an accountant to straighten out our operation. But we also realize that if we spend our budget on that person, much of our financial resources needed for the work we do will be gone. We need someone to come forward and volunteer. And we want a top quality professional, someone with a degree in accounting. How do we find that person? Well, the first step always is to figure out where that person is. Where does that person work, socialize, play? The best technique is to develop an informal think tank among your volunteers. Put three to five volunteers in a room and let everyone free associate as they brainstorm about all the places where they will find that person. Our accounting help is found at accounting firms, service clubs, church, golf clubs, university business schools, professional associations, homeowner groups, and on and on.

Once you lock on to one of these possibilities, then use the concept of *the beginning and the end*. Let's select that young university professor whose boss, the dean, said she needed some real world experience. You know that these young professors exist at your university and that they are in the business college, housed in the accounting department. But how do you approach them and ask for a professor to volunteer at your agency? You know it's a simple matter of asking, but who should you ask? Think about it. Who gains from your request? For one, the professor gains experience.

The dean and the university gains a better trained professor. Who has the most interest in this training? Well, the dean who hired this young professor is well aware of her lack of experience and might be the best one to twist an arm. If you approach the professor directly, you will probably hear that they are way too busy and that they need to get underway with their teaching. The older and more experienced dean would see the need for both the experience and, even more importantly, the connection that you offer to the university.

In fact, your organization offers visibility in the real world for that accounting department. And you offer internship possibilities for their seniors. Thinking further, your board of directors are important folks in the community and the dean would like to have a direct contact with them. What better way than to be offering the services of one of the university's best and brightest young professors? This may sound a little like, "What's in it for me again," and it is. Remember, that we all are looking to connect and network, and your organization is brewing with positive ways for people and organizations to share resources.

Same story for that well seasoned, highly knowledgeable professional about ready to retire. He or she needs to be motivated to volunteer for you. The same question then is applicable; who has the proper amount of knowledge of the person, who has the needed edge to get them to consider your request? Let's suggest we stay in our university example and target one of their senior professors. We know they have the ability and that they do consult with a number of Fortune 500s already. You offer one more opportunity for them to share their knowledge, this time as a volunteer. So, who should do the asking? Not their boss this time. That person, unless they are a close personal friend by now, does not have the personal clout to get a yes. In fact, that senior professor is starting to break away from the university and is seeking connections outside the university walls. Consider an associate from a professional association, a golfing buddy, or even an outstanding young graduate student who the professor has mentored for the past few years.

We have been discussing where to find these professionals and then, how to find the right person to do the ask. Think about it; each of us has a person in our lives, who when they ask a favor, we will drop everything to help. Each of us has a button and only a few people know how to push it. Once someone asks that individual, and the individual says no, it's no. I don't care who asks them after the first turndown, it's going to remain a no. So, it's very important that the right person does the initial ask. Don't waste that first opportunity. Assign the right person to conduct the ask. This may sound like a lot of work and planning for a simple ask. It is, but don't you really need the right person with the right experience? It is much better to spend your time locating that right person and then locating the right person to ask, than to be asking dozens of almost right people.

14

SKILLS, KNOWLEDGE, AND ATTITUDE

Dynamic leaders possess some distinguishing personality traits that give them the power and passion to succeed.

Warren Bennis

You may wonder what we look for in the potential volunteer. We look at the volunteer's skills, knowledge, and attitude (SKA). You know these topics very well. The S stands for *skills,* what the volunteer can do. Generally, this refers to hands-on skills. What kinds of skills do they possess? Can they keyboard on a computer, paint and handle a hammer, or draw and design a newsletter logo? We think about all the skills that a volunteer might have, and then consider which skills are needed for this particular job. What are their unique skills that the agency can use?

Then we look at the K, the volunteer's *knowledge* base. What does the volunteer know about? How can we make good use of their knowledge level? Are they a creative thinker? Can they train others to do tasks? Are they a strong communicator? What is their educational level? What specific training have they had in their work place that we might use? Knowledge is a very broad area and will require probing by you to locate all those interest areas that the volunteer might have. Most of us have much more knowledge than we apply everyday on the job. We sometimes limit our intake interview questions to that skill or knowledge that the volunteer uses everyday at work. So often, our avocational or hobby interests are even stronger and of more interest to us than that which we use in the job.

The third letter of the SKA is attitude. You might wonder why we consider the volunteer's attitude. Just how important is attitude? I really don't think you question how important having a positive attitude is to your volunteers, you know! All of us have had the misfortune of working with even one negative person. One person with a negative attitude can bring down all the motivation you try to instill into your organization. I think the best advice I've heard about working with negative people went like this; "I don't walk away from negative people. I run." Remember something you learned years ago, you can't change people. I always think of a friend of mine who fell in love with the nicest guy and she said to me one day, "I just love him, except for one small trait that drives me crazy, but I will get him to change that." You know that never happened. Even today, that trait is not only still there, it bothers her even more. I do not hire negative volunteers! They will destroy all that excitement and enthusiasm that is so necessary in the volunteer environment. And as stated, don't bother trying to change that person, they have spent all their life getting to where they are, and you can bet their spouse has also tried to change them.

Skills, knowledge and attitude, the three items that you need to search for as you interview the volunteer. You start by asking what the volunteer does for a living, their career skills, as well as what they do for their hobby interests. The workplace needs to inquire what sort of skills their people have and then allow them to move around the work place to use them. As you ask about these talents, jot them down on the back side of the volunteer application form as an aid to remember them.

Skills are usually hands on talents that volunteers have like photography, cooking, use of tools, etc. Ask questions about past employment and outside interests to gather this data. Many times the volunteers don't offer hobby interests, and that might just be their real passion.

Knowledge is different than skills. Knowledge is usually that information gathered by reading, conversing, or retained from school. It's the head knowledge of the volunteer that helps them work with a variety of tasks. I will ask what the volunteer majored in at college, what they enjoy reading about, and what their weekend activities involve. Gather data and write it down, again on the reverse side of your application. You are developing a composite view of your volunteer. All of this input will form a very different view of your volunteer than you will get from their application. The more you know about the volunteer, the better will be your ability to place the volunteer into the right job at the right place.

The skills and knowledge level of the volunteer is fairly easy to gather by questioning during normal conversation, but how do we gather information about their attitude? And why do we care about the attitude? Just teasing, I know you realize that the volunteer's attitude is one of the keys to their success in your place. Just one negative volunteer can create a difficult environment for other volunteers and yourself. I look for volunteers with a positive attitude.

One of the most exciting companies to work for in America is Southwest Airlines. It's a place where fun is a part of the everyday experience. As usual, at the great companies, it's the boss who really makes it happen. Past CEO Herb Kelleher is no exception. He sets the culture at Southwest by riding his Harley into the office and singing at the company parties. But it's Herb's comments about hiring staff members at Southwest that really sets the tone. He says that he knows how to hire, he hires for attitude and trains for skills. He notes in his book, *NUTS*, that you can easily train folks in the techniques of doing their jobs, but you can't really change their attitudes. Most negative people have spent most of their lives getting where their attitudes are. Nordstrom, that department store of legendary service, has found the same thing is true about their sales associates' attitudes. At Nordstrom they do not conduct smile training classes, they simply select the right people; people with good positive attitudes. When asked about how they train people to be so positive, they will tell you they don't, they let mom and dad do it! They simply select those people that mom and dad trained so well.

15

ONE SQUARE MILE

The significant problems we face cannot be solved at the same level of thinking we were at when we created them.

Albert Einstein

Many volunteers wish to volunteer at a place that has a real connection with who they are. This might be the hospital that took such loving care of the volunteer's mother. Or it might be the local Boy Scout troop where the volunteer once served as a scout. Or it might be the city where the volunteer lives and serves on the neighborhood watch team. This connection illustrates the Rule of One Square Mile.

All volunteers follow this Rule of the One Square Mile. That is, the volunteering opportunity must be within their personal one square mile. One square mile does not refer to a distance of a mile, it means there must be a closeness or connection between the volunteer and the goals of the volunteer organization. The heart of the volunteer must have a fit with the volunteer organization. Volunteers only volunteer for organizations that feel right for them and, usually, there is a close fit with their own past.

If the volunteer has had a loved one lost to a drunk driving accident, they will consider becoming a volunteer for Mothers Against Drunk Driving (MADD) or Dads Against Drunk Driving (DADD). University alumni will connect to do volunteer work for the university that they attended. The closer this connection the more likely the volunteer will say yes when asked. This connection is the law of the one square mile.

This rule does apply in a distance sense as well. Your fellow businesses located within a square mile of your agency location are much more likely to lend a hand on a project than groups located across town. The reason is clear, we support organizations that we can see and are located in our back yards. This means that the best places to ask for in-kind help, such as dinner for your special volunteer of the month and for printing help on that black tie dinner program, are the local merchants down the street. Why? Because they are within that one square mile. They are connected to you. They also realize that you will refer them to your volunteers when the volunteers are looking for their personal services. That's just good business common sense. By operating within your agency one square mile you are developing a relationship with the community. You might refer to this as relationship marketing, which it certainly is.

The rule of the one square mile applies within your organization as well. Think about the school or church volunteer program. Aren't you much more likely to attract volunteers from among those parents who have children attending your school than if they didn't have children at all? Why? Because they already have a connection with the organization. Same goes for church volunteer programs locating volunteers from among their members. It may seem like common sense, but it sometimes escapes us that your volunteers must have a tight connection with the purpose of your organization for them to volunteer and continue volunteering.

Sometimes we can create this rule of one square mile. Your activity in the community, becoming a member of organizations, service clubs, youth groups, will grow your circle of connections. Then when you are out trying to find collaborations between groups or volunteers for that one-time-a-year fund raiser, you have lots of people within your one square mile. People who you help and connect with will feel the desire to give back when you ask. You are out there working, but at the same time you are relationship building. People like to help people they know and organizations they understand and trust.

The one square mile rule also applies to the amount of publicity your group receives in the community. If people read about your organization it will produce a greater awareness of the group. The more people hear mention of your organization, the more likely they will say "yes" to someone asking them to volunteer. Remember that nobody ever volunteers for groups about which they know nothing. Try it sometime. Stand on your street corner and ask everybody walking by if they would be willing to volunteer for the Wicked Owl Society. I can tell you that you will get a wide variety of looks and comments, but no volunteers. People only volunteer for groups that they know about and respect. Volunteers have only so much time to give and they will be sure to give it where they know it will be well spent. Think about your own volunteer activities. Isn't that correct?

16

WHAT DO YOU EXPECT?

No man will make a great leader who wants to do it all himself, or to get all the credit for doing it.

Andrew Carnegie

All conversations with a new volunteer begin the same way, with you asking about the volunteer's expectations. I ask this simple question; what do you expect to receive from volunteering? Listen carefully to the answer, it will tell you how successful the volunteer relationship is going to be. If you can't meet the volunteer's expectation, the relationship will not work. Most volunteers respond with, "I just want to help the organization." Probe deeper. Ask about their reasons for selecting your specific organization. Volunteers have very specific expectations and they relate directly to the reason that you are their place to volunteer.

Expectations are as varied as the volunteers in your program. It's important to realize that volunteering is an exchange, both sides have expectations. We are careful to find out exactly what the volunteer expects, but we may not consider that we too have expectations. Our expectations need to be discussed with the volunteers as well.

My expectations might include their being on time for assignments, dressing in an appropriate fashion, being friendly, and having a customer service orientation. It might include proper handling of confidential information and having a positive attitude.

These expectations will be covered during orientation, but they should also be listed in your volunteer handbook. It's always a good idea to cover your expectations in a detailed way. Give your volunteers the opportunity to ask questions about your expectations. The volunteer's success depends on following these guidelines. These guidelines should be clear, well written, and easy to understand. There should be no confusion in the volunteer's mind concerning your expectations of their performance.

For example, if you have an expectation that the volunteer will honor confidentiality, that needs to be expressed. You need to explain that the volunteer might have access to student grade reports and other confidential information. Further, stress that their volunteer position requires this access, and you will train them in the proper use of this data. Sometimes the issue is that the volunteer does not understand that a dinner conversation with their spouse concerning this information would violate your confidentiality guidelines.

Another expectation might concern appropriate dress for your work place. The same issue might occur for paid employees. It is usually best to have a single dress standard for all staff, both paid and unpaid. Sometimes, a person might be planning to attend a party after work, and might wear something a little dressy for the office. While that person might be dressed for an evening event, they are not properly dressed for work.

Some folks might need suggestions as to what constitutes proper dress for your office. Sometimes people might under dress and arrive at their assignment without shoes or in jeans that have tears. We are concerned about the appearance of our volunteers because of how our clients might feel about the volunteer's dress. Dress standards should always reflect the audience served and the community. When in doubt, common sense is always an excellent guide.

Being on time is another expectation that you might hold. We may have strict time guidelines for paid staff and sometimes we are less concerned about volunteer tardiness. It is best to be consistent concerning all staff. When a volunteer is late, they are causing another volunteer to stay longer. This is a common reason for volunteers to become upset. When a volunteer waits for a tardy volunteer, and your volunteer has someplace to get to, we are creating a problem for them. Even if you take the shift, and wait for the tardy volunteer, your schedule is in disrepair, and it's not okay. Sure, all of us run into traffic some time, but we are concerned about those people who do not plan their day, anticipating problems, or worse yet, who might not care.

17

BOOT CAMP

We recruit what we are.

Major General Jack Klimp
U.S. Marine Corps

The U.S. Marines know quite a lot about volunteers. If fact, every young recruit and career officer in the corps is a volunteer. They recruit volunteers, train volunteers, and manage volunteers. If we are willing to look at their program, we will gain some interesting insights. Dan Carrison and Rod Walsh have written an interesting book titled *Semper Fi: Business Leadership the Marine Corps Way.* Recruiting in the Marine Corps is very different than in the other military branches.

Think about the average military recruiter in your local town. They are older men, usually nearing retirement age and not quite in top physical shape. They spin a tale for the young potential boys and girls about all the excitement the military offers. It appears that the recruiting officers will offer almost anything if the kids just sign on the dotted line. The only restriction tends to be that they want the youngsters to have had no trouble in their teen years and to have done well in high school.

The Marine recruiter is quite different, very strong, well-put-together, and dressed in their uniform without a wrinkle. In fact, it appears that this Marine might go to war at any moment. He is quite young, nowhere near retirement age. This Marine looks like The Few, The Proud, The Marines. The Corps does not actively recruit, the young people must be interested in joining. In *Semper Fi*, the authors quote Master Gunnery Sergeant Andy Brown, "We don't want warm bodies; we want commitment." Isn't this exactly what we want, commitment, rather than warm bodies? The Corps does not weed people out, they cultivate. They want people who want them. Regardless of what the recruit's background is, all they ask is that the recruit have commitment.

The quote at the top of this chapter says a lot about how recruiting really works. It says "We recruit what we are." John Maxwell, in his book, *The 21 Irrefutable Laws of Leadership,* calls this the law of magnetism. Maxwell says it clearly, "Leaders draw people who are like themselves." Organizations attract people with the same values, interests, and attitudes as the recruiters. That is exactly why the best recruiters you have are your outstanding, hard-working volunteers. They will bring in more people like themselves. They will be looking in the right places for the right people.

Another key task of the Corps is to create a ceremony of the first day. The day the new recruit arrives on the training base, the drill instructor, in full dress uniform, takes the recruit on a tour of the base. The recruit is told how important they are, what a good decision the new recruit has made and exactly what the training will involve. Our agencies also need to help our new volunteers to feel comfortable in their new surroundings. It is true that the first few days on the job as a new volunteer are the most critical to their retention. In customer service they refer to this first ex-perience as "the moment of truth." In his book, *At America's Service*, Karl Albrecht defines this moment of truth as " ...any episode in which the customer comes into contact with any aspect of the organization and gets an impression of the quality of its service." This happens with volunteers when they first walk into the school office as a parent volunteer. Did the secretary stop what she was doing to welcome them? Or did she act as if the volunteer was in the way, an extra burden for her day?

The attitude of staff toward volunteers is a critical part of the retention issue. Volunteers constantly express that one of the reasons they changed agencies is due to a lack of a friendly atmosphere at their last volunteer agency. Remember, volunteers don't really go away from volunteering, but they do, at times, go away from one organization and into another one. That's why an exit interview is helpful when a volunteer has asked to leave. At this point, you may find out a lot about your staff's attitude and how they impact volunteers. One negative staff member may create an exodus of volunteers. One day, while staying at a Hyatt Hotel, I passed a number of employees all wearing large buttons that stated "10 and 5". I had to know what that meant, and I asked a housekeeping staff member, and she was embarrassed to tell me. She said, "At Hyatt it is the rule that when a guest approaches you, within ten feet of the guest you must smile, and within five feet you say good day to them." She told me that this particular property had been found not observing this routine and they had to wear these buttons as a training tool. Sometimes we might need 10 and 5 buttons to remind us to recognize our volunteers. It's not that we don't honor and value the volunteers, it's usually that we are self-absorbed in the crisis of the moment.

The title of this chapter is Boot Camp, to indicate the importance of basic training. We conduct a type of boot camp, and it's called orientation. It's the first inside look at our organization for the new volunteer. In the Marine Corps, the new recruit learns the Marine Corps Way. In our organization, we want the new volunteer to learn the agency way. We all have policies and procedures for doing the job, and it's important to pass this on to the volunteers. The Marine Corps gives us an interesting concept to consider; they refer to basic training as transformation time. Transformation is the purpose of boot camp. It changes the young recruit for life. The authors in *Semper Fi* said it best, in a poster recruiting for the

Corps. It said, "maybe all one needs to have is an earnest attitude and good character, the Marine Corps will supply the rest."

Our orientation serves the same purpose as the Corps boot camp, that is to standardize policies and procedures. Orientation is to make everyone into believers, to share the corporate values, and to deliver your agency stories. It is important to start everyone at the same place, to insure that everyone is reading from the same page. Your orientation is the formal introduction of the new volunteer to your agency and to their job. It's very interesting that new volunteers remember their orientation for years to come. They are excited and ready to start when they attend your orientation. Your purpose in orientation should be to make your new volunteers feel that they made the correct decision in selecting your volunteer place.

Orientation should be a process, not a program. It should be on-going, with training available at regular intervals. Too many organizations do an orientation and assume that the volunteers are trained for life. You should consider that training continues to maintain volunteer productivity and alignment with your organization's mission. In her book, *Volunteer Program Administration*, Joan Kuyper states that "orientation... should emphasize how much the agency values the volunteer program and what volunteers have accomplished." It is a good idea to involve others in the orientation program. Successful volunteers give an inside view of the volunteer program to the new recruit. Your boss, and the agency director, should be involved in welcoming the new volunteers. This lets the new folks know that the top leadership in your organization honors the value of volunteers. You are building an on-going relationship with these new volunteers, and orientation is the start of this relationship between the agency and the new volunteer.

18

EMPOWER YOUR VOLUNTEERS

*The first responsibility of a leader is to define reality. The last is to say
thank you. In between the two, the leader must become a servant and
debtor. That sums up the progress of an artful leader.*

Max De Pree

One of those business terms you hear all the time these days is empowerment. I must have twenty books on my shelf with that word right in the
title. But what does empowerment mean, and how might it apply to my
volunteer program? To me, empowerment means the two capital T's, that
is Training and Trust. You must train the volunteers to do their assignment correctly. Correctly means doing it correctly and doing it your way.
We all have our own way of performing a task, and we do not feel okay if
it's not done just that way. The second T is trust. Once you have trained
the volunteer, why not trust them to do it?

Part of the frustration I hear from volunteers is, "they give me a job,
but they never really let me do it!" "They are always checking on me, it's
so disturbing, don't they trust me?" See, the very point of empowering

someone is to train them first and, once trained, trusting them to perform the way you trained them. It would be silly to trust a volunteer if you had not spent the time showing them the proper way to do the assignment. It would be just as silly to take the time to train them but fail to trust them to do the job.

The best story that I have heard to illustrate the concept of empowerment centers around that institution of legendary service, Nordstrom. Nordstrom is the customer service legend. Most professional speakers on customer service use Nordstrom stories. Here's one now. The gentleman walks into Nordstrom and he is carrying two tires. He puts the tires on the counter and he says, "I am not happy with these tires." Mary, the Nordstrom sales associate, asks him how much he paid for them. He says, "Two hundred dollars." She reaches in the cash drawer and gives the gentleman the money, and he leaves the store with a smile on his face. The sales associate standing next to Mary says, "Mary, we don't sell tires!" Mary says, "It doesn't matter, the customer is happy." Silly, maybe, but the point it makes is real solid gold Nordstrom. It is reported that Bruce Nordstrom heard this story and remarked that he didn't know if it was true or just another of those legendary Nordstrom fables, but, he said, "If it happened, I hope it was handled just like the story."

The key to the Nordstrom tire story is not about taking back tires. It's about the feeling of Mary the Nordstrom sales associate, who knew that anything she did to help a customer would be okay with management, so long as the customer was happy. That's how it should be with our volunteers also. So long as we select the right volunteers, train them to do the job our way, place them in the correct position for their skill level and attitude, why not trust them to perform? Sometimes it's our fears and insecurities that lead us to always second-guess our staff members.

How do we instill into our volunteers the ability to make decisions without our standing over them? According to Robert Spector, in his book, *The Nordstrom Way*, "What separates Nordstrom from its competitors is it's army of highly motivated, self-empowered people who have an entre-preneurial spirit, who feel that they're in this to better themselves and to feel good about themselves...and to be successful." Bruce Nordstrom told Morley Safer on *60 Minutes*, "These sales people have the opportunity to be successful because Nordstrom gives its employees the freedom to make decisions. And Nordstrom management is willing to live with those deci-sions." Let's try to Nordstromize our volunteer programs with this type of empowerment. I am always so excited when visiting a hospital gift shop and the sales person acts as if they are running their own business. It re-minds me of that old time saying that refers to empowerment as letting the inmates run the institution. In Spectors' book, Jammie Baugh, the general manager of Nordstrom's Southern California region is quoted as saying, "At Nordstrom, we do want the inmates to run the asylum."

19

THINK STAFF!

We make a living by what we do, but we make a life by what we give.

Winston Churchill

Whenever I visit a volunteer place and talk to the program director, I listen for that "word." I call it the "problem" word. It's the word "professional," and it's used this way; "We have four professional staff and two hundred amateur volunteers." Okay, they may not use the word "amateur," but the meaning is there anyway. Think about it, what does it say? Are the only professionals in an agency the paid people? I have never had a volunteer that wasn't a professional. Every volunteer has skills, knowledge, and talents that allow him/her to perform at a professional level. I know that the person using the term "professional staff" doesn't mean it as a demeaning term, but it might sound that way to the volunteer.

If you treasure volunteers, and select them carefully, you need to consider them as professionals in your program. Apply the correct label to your valuable help. Call them "staff members." You then have both paid and unpaid staff, but call them both staff members. Don't get confused by this. It's true that being a volunteer is having an honored title. But they are truly a support staff member for your team. I realize that we have a varied level of professionals working in all organizations. Some people hold degrees, some are state licensed, a few are certified, and so on. I am not attempting to remove any credibility from these hard working members of your team. But everyone on your team is there to support each other and they all deserve the title of staff member.

At times, your volunteers might even wish to be called volunteer staff members. Many times your seniors actually prefer to be recognized by the term volunteer. I have never had a senior volunteer object to the title volunteer staff member. I find it's a way of honoring the work and effort of the volunteer when you add the title "staff" to their name badge or business card. It is a simple way to show the value of the volunteers to the program. At times it might be your other staff members that object to this new title of staff being applied to the volunteers. They may see it as a degradation to their paid positions. In that case, you need to discuss openly at a meeting of all paid and unpaid staff members the important purpose of the volunteers at your place.

Sometimes, even the age of your volunteers will make a difference in how they wish to be titled. I have worked with police department volunteers and noticed this difference. The younger volunteers, usually Explorer Scouts, want to have everyone think of them as full staff members. They want the public to view them as police officers. They want the same uniform, the same vehicles, the same staff titles. They want to be seen exactly the same as the people they work alongside. The senior members of the team, usually members of the Retired Senior Volunteer Program (RSVP) want the world to recognize them as volunteers. These seniors are upset if their badges don't say "volunteer staff".

It is important to avoid any problems between your paid and unpaid staff by making it clear as to the reason that you have volunteers. Volunteers are never hired to replace paid staff. You hire paid staff to perform critical jobs and they are selected and retained based on their ability to perform a critical specific task. They might be licensed, certified, or credentialed by a board to perform these tasks. We are not replacing paid employees with volunteers. But, at times, I have seen paid staff feel this. We work very hard explaining to our employee unions that we have no such plans. But that still may not remove the fear that paid staff members hold when the volunteers arrive. Make it very clear that your volunteers are there to support the paid staff. This is a critical issue to discuss openly with your paid staff. They need to understand the purpose of your volunteer program. They need to realize that you honor and respect the paid staff. Bringing volunteers into your work place needs to be, in part, to support those paid staff members. Volunteers are there to support them in their work.

Another reason to always address your volunteer staff by the term staff is that it is self esteem building for the volunteers. It allows the volunteer staff to feel that the agency values their contribution by assigning them a meaningful title. They will begin to feel like a cohesive member of your team. Team building is a difficult process to carry out inside a non-profit agency. And one critical step in team building is to allow everyone to feel honored and treasured as a member. A simple title, the title "Staff," even accompanied by the term paid or unpaid, will help build a feeling of connection.

It is important for us to consider the volunteers as staff members, if your selection process is professional. Don't you work as hard to locate volunteers as you do your paid employees? You select both team members after a search based on a job description. You look at each person's capabilities, skills, knowledge level, and good attitude. Each person, once hired, is in a probational status, is trained to improve performance, and is evaluated on a regular basis. You do not accept anything but top performance from your staff and you both reward outstanding performance and coach toward continually improved performance. If this is true, and all team members add to your organization's bottom line, then why not consider all personnel as a part of your staff?

20

A RESOURCE AND A STRATEGY

The man who kindly guides a stranger on his way, lights as were another's lantern from his own nor light the less for kindling the other.

Cicero

Volunteers are a resource when you consider the fantastic collection of skills and talents that they bring to us. Even if I had the money to hire additional paid staff, I would not have this selection of talent. In fact, paid staff are more alike than different in many ways. We usually come from the same type of training places, with fairly common sorts of backgrounds. One college graduate with a background in social services fairly well matches the next graduate in skill level. But, your volunteers come from all walks of life, one will be a retired nurse and the next an active accountant.

When we consider the types of help we get from our volunteers, we usually just think about the physical hands-on help. While very important, we also must consider the thinking aspect of our volunteer staff. At times in my volunteer career, I have been lucky enough to have what I called my "volunteer think tank." This was a group of outstanding individuals;

my most recent group were all early retired management types who did nothing for us but think. They would meet weekly for an hour and over a morning cup of coffee would discuss our marketing and business plans in detail. These were my equivalent of a group of highly paid consultants in marketing. They were each experts, having worked all their lives in the business arena, and now they were supplying the results of all that experience to us.

Volunteers are a strategy for connecting with our larger community and volunteers are wonderful at connecting. This resource of volunteer help can do so much more for us than just the physical or thinking work. This corps of volunteers is our support system and public relations vehicle in the community. This group attends the city council meetings, talks up our needs, and finds us the support we need out there. Every volunteer represents this support to you, but we may overlook the training it takes to produce a really viable force. Every volunteer talks to dozens of people every day. Every volunteer is excited about the work the agency does. Make this corps of volunteers work for you 24 hours a day. The secret to having every volunteer become a proactive public relations team is to let them know just how important this work is. Think about a school district going through a bond issue election. The community needs to know about the needs of the district so they will rally around and pass that bond. You might place a few paid newspaper advertisements and put up a group of posters and even hand out flyers to all the local merchants. But this activity is nothing compared to your volunteers talking to everyone they know. They talk to people where they work, where they shop, to friends and relatives. Each volunteer is a one-person band of support and because they are so excited, people listen to them. One volunteer with passion can convince hundreds of others to join your crusade.

This plan to produce a team that connects with the larger community, to get the word out, requires training your volunteers in the best ways to use their public relations talents. One excellent training tool for helping volunteers understand how to get the word out is a book by Michael

Levine, *Selling Goodness*. This book will serve as a guide for promoting your non-profit organization. This book suggests that getting money for your organization is only half the battle; the other half is "getting the world to hear your message, and assimilate it into their hearts." This maxim, Levine says, "hits on the same distinction about giving a man a fish versus teaching a man to fish." His thoughts reflect what we have been discussing about the value of getting all those volunteers with passion out there into the community delivering your well crafted message.

21

THE RECRUITING TEAM!

The speed of the boss is the speed of the team.

Lee Iacoca

I don't like recruiting committees. If you select a group of your volunteers to recruit other volunteers for the organization, it removes that responsibility from everyone else. If people know that a committee is busy at work finding new volunteers, then they don't feel it's their job. That's the problem. It is everyone's responsibility to continually be thinking about finding new volunteers. But when you set out to find the key leadership players, that's where a recruiting team makes sense.

Locating your key players for leadership roles is difficult. One reason that people hesitate to take on meaningful positions is that if they do an outstanding job as a black tie dinner chair this year, it will be assumed that they will do it again next year. The assumption that all good leaders will be willing to continue to repeat being leaders over and over again is the key to why people say no. One rule that I follow in recruiting leadership is that leaders are not allowed to assume the same leadership role more than once. This allows someone to work hard at a position without fear of becoming a chair for life. But, once you serve in a leadership role such as the black-tie dinner chair, you are expected to help select your replacement. Therefore, the ex-chairs become alumni of the position and will come together to select the next black-tie dinner chair.

Finding the right person for a leadership position requires a unique thought process. Step one involves the process of conducting a task analysis. A task analysis involves looking at the skills and knowledge required by the position you are seeking to fill. Let's use the position of black-tie dinner chair. This chair position requires a person with abilities in organization and influence. The chair needs to influence others to raise money, contact vendors for gifts, and organize the invitation activities. People work for people and the leader has a lot to do with who is willing to serve on all the committees required for a successful black-tie dinner.

The people who have been recent chairs are an excellent recruiting team because they have been there and done it. They know exactly how much work the job entails and especially which skills to look for in the new chair. They can also discuss those items and procedures that caused them a concern when they were chairs. This group serves as an advisory group both to you, as director, and to the incoming chair. And with this system, the incoming chair is aware that it is only a one-time position and they realize that they will be helping to select their replacement. This task of selecting their replacement is generally a stress-free job and, in fact, becomes a social hour as these individuals have a chance to review the fun and frustrations they had with the position. You might suggest a lunch or dinner get-together for three of the most recent chairs as an opportunity to discuss this search for the new chair.

I suggest that this team follow the fundraising model of prospect, cultivate, and ask as a tool to help them locate the best volunteer to fill this position. Step one involves the prospecting for that person best suited to become this year's chair. They usually start with our membership or volunteer roster and discuss each person's abilities and current positions.

They might look at current and past board members, officers and commit-tee heads. The tasks involved in doing this job are discussed and might even be ranked as to their importance. This brainstorming concerning just what skills might be helpful, and what skills each past chair might have felt would have helped them, is of prime importance in the selection of the new chair.

Combing this list of potential candidates should involve the volunteer director and the executive director of the agency. Each person has had experiences with the potential volunteer being considered and will be able to give much needed insight. At some point following this task analysis and gathering of input concerning the candidates abilities, a decision will be reached to make the final selection. Step two concerns itself with cul-tivating the potential candidate and following it with asking the person to accept the position. Cultivation means nothing more than presenting the candidate with all the information required for them to make a decision concerning their own time constraints and interest to take on this type of assignment.

The key to getting the selected person to accept the position is best accomplished by having the best person ask. It's true that each of us has a person in our lives who, if they asked for a favor, you would drop the world to help. Our task is to insure that we select the most appropriate person to conduct the ask. You can imagine in your own life individuals who might ask you to take on a position, and just the person asking might cause you to say no thanks. The recruiting team needs to consider indi-vidually who has the most influence over your candidate in the decision of accepting this leadership role. Sometimes this involves discussing the position with the candidates spouse or adult children. It might be a best friend that could influence the candidate to consider the role.

This process might seem to you like overkill, or at least a large amount of effort simply to select one leadership volunteer. But, consider the harm that can be done by selecting the wrong person to head up an activity like the fundraising black-tie dinner special event. The wrong person might leave at mid-stream, lack enthusiasm, or simply not have the ability to carry out the duties. In any case, you must have the best leadership person to allow for a successful social and fundraising event.

22

MOTIVATION AND COMMITMENT

There are two things people want more than sex and money...
Recognition and praise.

Mary Kay Ash

Policies and procedures. Rules and regulations. Motivation and commitment. These pairs of words are confusing to most people. Just exactly what do they mean? Can you really differentiate policies from procedures? Can you distinguish rules from regulations? Most people have the same problem defining motivation and commitment. But there is a real difference between these words in the volunteer place.

In my seminars, I use the following example of the difference between motivation and commitment. Assume you are the volunteer coordinator for a major university, working to gather alumni to serve on your volunteer team. You have a license frame on your car that states that you are an alumnus of Great University. It further states that your university mascot is the butterfly. At a stop light down the road you spot a car wearing the same license plate frame. You pull up at the light and ask the person in that other car to roll down their window so you can speak to them. They do and you introduce yourself as the volunteer director at the Great University. You ask if they are an alumnus and therefore a candidate for your volunteer program. They say yes, that they, in fact, are a fellow butterfly. You yell, "Go Butterflies," and they do the same. You then ask if they would be willing to volunteer for the Great University and they hit the gas and roar away. You are confused by this behavior and therefore you desire to catch them at the next stoplight and talk more. At the next light you ask why they rushed away when you asked about their volunteering. They tell you directly that they paid a large sum of money to attend the Great University and they have no plans to give of themselves for free. You ask them if they are committed to the Great University. They yell out the Butterfly fight song and end with a strong, "Go Butterflies!" This person is highly committed to their university, but they are not motivated to volunteer at all.

It is very common to find people who believe very strongly in the cause you represent. They will tell you how proud they are of the work that your organization performs. They tell you to keep up the good work, but that they are not personally interested in volunteering themselves for the organization. You see they are very committed to the cause but not at all motivated to do anything. So, while commitment is a very desirable value in people, it will not always translate into any work. at all. It is more a belief being announced than a desire to truly help out.

Of course, our best volunteers have both a strong commitment to the organization and a strong motivation to help with the tasks at hand. Given the choice, I will always look for motivated volunteers to get the work done. But there is something very important in this concept of commitment. I used to worry about offering additional work or an opportunity to chair a committee to my volunteers. I thought giving volunteers more work, or even a promotional opportunity, might burn them out. I was amazed. Almost always, those volunteers with additional work, or those accepting the committee chair position, became more committed to us. Could it be that those volunteers more involved with the organization also grew in the level of commitment to the organization?

That is exactly what happens to volunteers. Think about your own volunteer involvement. Didn't you take on more and more responsibility and, at the same time, grow in commitment? I always listen for the language of the volunteers to grow as well. I begin to hear the volunteer saying, "We are the best organization," or "we have the best program in town." It's the "we" word that indicates growth in volunteer commitment.

Think about those times in your life when you were really happy with a job, and you went home telling your family that we make the best product or have the best service. The volunteer does the same thing; they change from "they" to "we." New volunteers usually are told what the organization does, its mission as what we do to help people. They also tell others as new volunteers that "they do the following good deeds to help people." But after a while, and much hard work, you will hear the volunteer say, "We do much hard work." This change in language from "they" to "we" indicates a growth in the volunteer's commitment.

If motivation is what we are looking to produce in our volunteers, how do we do it? Many authors state that motivation cannot be produced by someone else, it must come from within. It's believed that you can't motivate others, that you can only motivate yourself. You might be able to force one to do something, but coercion will not lead to a sense of commitment. One long-standing story about motivation says, "If you tell someone what you'll give him for doing something, that's called an incentive; if you tell someone to do something or else he'll get fired, it's called motivation."

Corporate leaders have given up the control mode of authority and have moved toward an empowerment mode where employees become associates rather subordinates. This creates an environment where staff can be motivated. This new environment eliminates negative consequences and uses praise and recognition as tools for motivation. These motivators work in the volunteer place as well. Motivation for volunteers includes recognition and praise for work done well, challenging work assignments and volunteer growth opportunities.

Recognition and praise must be spontaneous, timely and given for outstanding performance. Challenging assignments must involve work that the volunteer sees as meaningful, worthwhile. Volunteer growth opportunities include the chance to attend seminars and receive books and audiotapes on subjects related to their volunteer assignments.

23

NO. VS NO,

The first and perhaps the final test of leadership is your ability to attract and keep followers.

John C. Maxwell

This is a strange title for a book chapter, No. vs No,. But think about the last time you were asked to take on a project or accept a leadership role in a volunteer organization. You either wanted to take that assignment on or you didn't. Either you had an interest in it or you didn't. Either you had enough time to do it or you didn't. Either you knew enough about the subject to do a good job or you didn't. Right? If you listened to yourself as you told the person no, you would have heard either a no. or a no,.

If you said no period (no.), you were indicating that this was final, you did not want this job or you did not have the time in your schedule to do it correctly. What did the person that was asking you do? They probably started working you toward reconsideration or worse, they started begging and pleading. How did you feel? Guilty? Angry? Confused? Maybe you reconsidered and said okay, you would take the job. How did you do?

Probably not as well as you would have if you had either interest or time, right? The problem was that the person doing the ask didn't know the difference between no. and no,.

The real problem with this lack of awareness about the no. and no, is that the best volunteer will feel guilty and take on an assignment that they don't have interest or time for. And then they do an okay job, but feel like they have let you down. They may be your best volunteer, but you are offering them an assignment after they told you that they really don't want it or have the time to do it 100%. Once they fail to carry the task to the quality that they know is expected, you have a chance of losing that volunteer. Think about that. You get a halfway result and chance losing your best volunteer. Isn't it simpler to listen when they say no?

When the volunteer says no, it might indicate that they don't feel they have been around your organization long enough to accept that level of assignment. You must feel they are capable of performing, so go ahead and beg. By beg I mean tell them that you feel they have the talent to complete the task to your satisfaction. Or, the volunteer might feel they need additional training to do a good job. If so, tell them that you will send them to a seminar or hook them up with a co-chair that has more experience in that area.

The unstated key to success with these no, volunteers is to find out exactly what their hesitation is. Do they just feel insecure? Or are they doubting their ability? Or do they feel that they are not well enough connected in the organization to get others to join their team? All of these feelings are things that you can help with. But the important item that you need to find out is does the volunteer have enough time to take on this task. If the volunteer truly states that she does not have enough time, that is a no. Listen to a no period.

The two keys to a volunteer's success is that the volunteer have both the time and the talent to take on that leadership role. You can help with enhancing their talent bank, but usually time is a dead end street for you. If your volunteer has no spare time, because of career or family, there's not much you can do to help.

24

VOTE WITH YOUR FEET

*A positive attitude is like a bank account. You can't continually
draw on it without making deposits.*

Wolf J. Rinke

Volunteers do vote with their feet! Unlike employees who only leave
after receiving their final pay check, volunteers just leave. When a volunteer is unhappy with the way they are treated, they can just disappear.
It's important to consider the things that cause a volunteer to feel so
upset that they will even consider leaving the volunteer place. It's really
no different for paid staff, it usually comes down to common sense and
niceness.

One example from my volunteer life might help here. As a volunteer
with an agency, I was involved with organizing a large black-tie dinner.
I had worked three years on this project and had yet to be thanked for
my work, even though the volunteers were thanked on a regular basis. I
noticed the fact that I was never sent thank you notes or given the verbal
thanks by the paid volunteer director. I did wonder why, since I was in
charge of the entire event and all the other paid and volunteer staff were

getting their work assignments from me. I was the boss, the person in control of the success or failure of this large activity. I thanked my support staff of volunteers, but somehow the boss never thought to thank me.

My wife, Ann, and I were flying recently and during a lunch at 36,000 feet, it came to me. I had an eye opening thought and I said to Ann, "I know why I haven't been thanked for my leadership role on that black-tie dinner." She looked at me and said "Oh, here it comes." I said "We look too much like the boss, or at least we look like paid employees." I was wearing a pager, a cell phone, carrying the clip board and telling everyone what to do; I was in charge. You know the answer, how often does the boss get thanked, or even, how often do the paid staff members get thanked? Think about it. When was the last time you got a thank you note from your boss?

Sad, but true. We thank the volunteers, but forget to thank the paid staff. One very interesting sidelight to this thought concerns our board. Your board is made up of very dedicated, wonderful volunteers that give hours of time to the operation of your agency every month. And yet this board is also in the role of being the boss. The board passes on most budget items, and makes decisions on employing staff. See the issue? They are both volunteers and the boss. Just as I was when I ran that black-tie dinner, I was a volunteer and was in complete charge of the event. I made decisions concerning expenditures and even assigned volunteers and paid staff to various roles for the event. I was volunteer and boss, so why did I think I would be thanked?

When we hold retreats for board members, a regular part of our training activities, I always hear from the board members the same thought. They say, " We are respected and listened to everyday, but we are seldom thanked for our efforts." I don't mean hosting a thank you dinner for the board. These dinners are nice and needed recognition activities, but the real thank you needs to come in a spur of the moment fashion. From your heart, the board members and paid staff need to hear and read a sincere thank you.

Usually it's small but important, things that frustrate volunteers enough for them to consider leaving your volunteer place. The lack of appreciation is of prime importance, of course, but only one of many reasons. A second reason is the lack of concern for the volunteer's time. The volunteer comes in to your place and you do not have the work ready for him/her to start, or worse, you forget that he/she was coming in this morning. She/he arrives and you rush around trying to find anything for him/her to do, kind of a busy work session. The volunteer is very aware of when you are organized by producing meaningful work and when you are giving them something to keep them busy. It would be smarter to call the volunteer and admit that you are not ready yet for his/her help than to allow him/her to come in and then waste his/her time. Nothing irritates volunteers like someone wasting their volunteer time.

Another frustration to volunteers is assuming that they want to do a certain assignment, without asking first. You might be able to assign a task to a paid staff member but don't try that with a volunteer. Asking the volunteer if a certain assignment would interest them before assigning it goes a long way to creating a good relationship with the volunteer. Avoid thinking "warm body" where everyone is "just a volunteer" and interested in doing anything as long as it helps the agency. Yes, many volunteers will do just about anything to help the organization. They love both the volunteer place and the clients or mission the agency serves, but they also wish to enjoy their time with you. Asking their opinion before assigning a task is just good sense. Even a paid staff member enjoys being asked, not told, before being assigned a job.

25

MBWA

When I see a thick manual, I know I'm looking at a slow company,
one that's struggling under a lot of excess baggage.

Tom Peters

Thanks to that management guru, Tom Peters, the author of a whole group of successful management books, including the classic *In Search of Excellence*, for this chapter's theme. Managing By Wandering Around, or MBWA, indicates that you are aware of everything that is going on in your place, while you are focused on everything at the same time.

I first saw this concept in action during a visit to one of our favorite eateries, Macaroni Grille. They are an interesting learning establishment; by that I mean just watch their management in action some night. You will see the guy with the tie doing everything. He is clearing tables, serving food, greeting guests, and even sweeping the floor. His job is not waiter or bus boy or custodian, nor does he own the place. He is simply doing whatever it takes to make the place work. How many times during a nice dinner are you left with empty soup bowls sitting in front of you and your dinner mate for twenty minutes? This MBWA manager would have noticed them and removed them with a friendly greeting as well. If your steak is ready but your wait person is occupied by another guest, this manager knew it was ready and simply served it to you. No big deal, just doing whatever needs to be done. No comments such as, "That's not my job!".

The volunteer coordinator is excellent at this MBWA approach. He or she is aware of all the activities going on in the volunteer place, just as the manager at my Macaroni Grille was paying attention to everything. But it's the wandering around aspect that really pays dividends. By wandering, you are meeting the volunteers on a regular basis, giving praise whenever it's needed and coaching on a regular basis to continually improve performance.

This ability I am discussing of focusing on everything at one time reminds me of a wood shop teacher I had in junior high school. He was in a room full of 40 kids, dust, and noise, complete chaos. But he was so tuned in to his environment that in the midst of all that activity, he heard one sound that indicated that a student was mis-feeding wood into the table saw and he yelled "stop" just in time to avoid an injury.

Focusing and wandering around at the same time. That may seem to be opposites, asking you to be both focused and aware of the big picture at the same time. With a little practice, you will find that wandering around helps you gain focus and an overall view while allowing you to listen to and observe details. Too many managers spend their time in offices and literally never enter the shop.

You may feel that if you are always wandering around, the volunteers may think you are checking up on them. This may be a risk, but my experience is different in that I find my volunteers enjoy both a chance to chat about their activities as well as having an opportunity to observe you doing real work as well.

Part of the opportunity to have volunteers observe you in the trenches means that you are the model for them to learn from. As you greet a guest at the front counter at City Hall or as you ask if you can help the customer in the hospital gift store, you are a model. You can conduct customer service training in the training room, but I can tell you that it's really learned on the front line. By MBWA you are given a front line view of how well your volunteers are performing. If you see a volunteer showing a negative attitude or being a little impatient with a guest, you have the perfect time to fix the problem. You are there on the line with them. You might suggest that the two of you take a few minutes to get a cup of coffee and then your opportunity to praise or coach presents itself.

Too many managers write up the staff member and then wait until performance review time to bring out those negative observations. It is their way of fixing that person's performance. The best time to improve performance is right when it happens. I call that method of praising and coaching "spur of the moment consultation". That is, by dealing with the issue right now it has the most impact on the person. You might try a little bit of MBWA. I think you will have your eyes opened to both how well your staff performs and, on occasion, you will spot those coaching moments available to you.

26

LEADERSHIP 101

*Every leader needs a flight plan since leading means doing the right
things, and managing means doing things right.*

Warren Bennis

Much has been written about leadership versus management. In the volunteer field, we usually talk about managing volunteers and our role as a manager of volunteers. Warren Bennis, in his recent book with a fun title, *Managing People Is Like Herding Cats*, stresses that most organizations are over-managed and under-led. Warren feels that too much attention is being paid to doing things right and not enough to doing the right things. This is talking about understanding the difference between what's urgent and what's important. I worked for an organization once that installed a new voice mail system. The system allowed a caller to add an urgent message to your voice mail by inserting this new "urgent" message ahead of all the other messages waiting to be heard. You know, I have never received an "urgent" message that was important!

Leaders always ask questions, important questions. One question asked by most leaders is "What's important around here?", That's a very

important and necessary question. It assumes that not everything is equally important; that you must make decisions and set priorities about things.
If you take the time to think about what's important and then spend your
time on the most important things, positive things will happen. Stephen
Covey, in his book, *First Things First*, shows us the need to define what is
truly important. Most people worry about time-management systems in
order to get things done, but actually they really work hard avoiding important things. Procrastination usually means doing the easy things and
avoiding the important items on their list of to-dos. It is a good strategy in
working with volunteers to have a small group of volunteers sit down and
brainstorm answers to that question, what's important around here. They
will be amazed that many of the day to day activities they are involved
with are not critical to the success of the organization. They will also find
out that they are taking on tasks which, while useful and worthwhile, may
not be critical to the organization's mission. We do a lot of things without
considering whether we are doing things right or if we are doing the right
things.

Think again about that concept of being over-managed and under-
led. Isn't it true that we spend a lot of time writing new policies, developing practices and even updating our volunteer handbooks? On the
face of it, there is nothing wrong with these things. Volunteer programs
need policies and ground rules and every program should have a handbook. But we need to insure that we spend time on issues like vision,
empowerment, and trust. Policies and handbooks are not going to build
a strong, creative, non-profit agency. People build an outstanding organization, not policies or handbooks. At times, I look into the American
Sign Language dictionary to help me find meanings in words and again,
this time it didn't let me down. The sign for manager is to put both your
hands out in front of you and pull them in toward yourself, as in holding
the reins of a horse with both hands. I think you can see that when you do
that with any animal you are attempting to control the animal. The sign
for manager then, is one who controls another. Their sign for leading is

putting your arms together and cradling them in front of you as if you are holding a baby in your arms. To lead then, is to nurture the other person. I find it so eye-opening that managing tends to be controlling and leading is a form of nurturing.

Think about your own past work experiences. Haven't you had bosses that used control as a management tool? Almost using fear, fear of losing your job, or fear of not getting a pay raise. While these techniques might get the job done, they do not build feelings of pride or positive attitudes. You have also had bosses who allowed you to perform at your own pace, giving you praise and coaching you when you needed it most. We tend to enjoy that style of leadership and tend to avoid bosses that use the controlling management style, right? Too often, the manager has her eyes on the bottom line, thinking about pushing ahead, getting things done, rather than seeing the bigger picture. The bigger picture is that people who are trusted and nurtured want to do their job and do not need someone standing over them. Leadership is about efficiency, management is about being effective. The leader that trusts the volunteer or staff member is allowing them to be efficient, to flow with their own internal time clock, and in so doing is empowering them toward success.

The second important question that leaders always ask is, "where are we headed?". The answer to that question must always be toward someplace better than where we are today. Can you imagine an organization that day-by-day gets worse, gives less service, builds a lower quality product? But you realize, that's what happens in some organizations. Leaders focus on improving every day, learning how to do tasks better, and producing a better product or improving service. Leaders refer to this kind of organization as a learning organization, a kind of place where everyone strives to grow every day. Leaders know where the organization is headed and what it will take to get it there. Leaders are aware that supporting the status quo, doing the same thing day in and day out will create a stale place. One way leaders drive this engine of continual change is by always expressing their dreams or visions. These dreams are exciting and serve to rally people around them. Leaders can clearly articulate their vision for the organization. This vision must be communicated.

Change is a scary topic for many of us. Leaders that ask about direction, with questions inquiring about where are we headed, ask questions about change. Every leader needs to accept that change is critical to every organization. The most difficult role of a leader is getting others to accept that change is growth. One of the strongest strengths that a leader must have is being an active change agent for the organization.

The third question that leaders always ask is, **"what do we stand for?"**. This question hits right at the values of the organization. It speaks to the need for every organization to be value-driven. It speaks to knowing the purpose of the organization. It speaks to using organizational values to further the organization's purpose. It's important to look at those framed value statements usually found on the wall of the organization. See if the organization is living them or just letting them gather dust. How many organizations talk about the fact that people count, but the reality tends to be that all decisions come down from above?

One of the keys to helping an organization strengthen and transmit its values is to insure that the leaders use influence to enable volunteers and staff to accomplish goals. John Maxwell, in his book, *The 21 Irrefutable Laws of Leadership,* discusses the importance of influence. John says, "You will never be able to lead if you don't have influence". He discusses Princess Diana and comments that people may not have thought of her as a leader, but that she did make things happen because she was an influencer. He says, "Leadership is influence, nothing more, nothing less." In defining influence, Maxwell relates a story that we can all understand. He uses the E.F. Hutton television commercials to illustrate the power of influence. In the commercial, the setting is a restaurant full of people talking to each other, when a person at one table says, "Well, my broker is E.F. Hutton, and E.F. Hutton says..." At that point, everybody in the restaurant turns toward this one table and listens to what this person has to say. John Maxwell calls this the *Law of E.F. Hutton.* In other words, when the real leader speaks, people do listen.

27

BECOME A COACH

You've got to believe deep inside yourself that you're destined
to do great things.

Joe Paterno

The volunteer place, at times, resembles an athletic arena, with terms such as team building, playing for success, winning the game, and coaching being the current jargon. Why are we trying to relate the volunteers to team players and the volunteer coordinator to a coach? Simply because the concept makes a lot of sense. Volunteers do want to win the game, and the game is the result of all their volunteer activity. Volunteers are serious about their activities and they want to see results from their efforts. The metaphor of the winning team and the coach as a leader does have a place in the volunteer setting. Warren Bennis, in writing the preface to John Robinson's book, *Coach To Coach*, states that a coach has a unique job. He says that, "Unlike most other positions where an individual seeks to gain recognition through personal achievement and accomplishment, the coach's success is based on an ability to inspire others to high performance and success." This is exactly the role that we seek as a volunteer coach.

The role of being a coach has many dimensions. Don Shula, NFL coach, says that, "Your job (as a coach) is to instruct, discipline, and inspire them to do things better than they could do on their own." These are the programs that we use everyday with our volunteers; training, recognition, and praise to support them, and just spending the time to get to know them better. Coaching is really about building volunteer commitment. It is about employing strategies for improving performance through commitment. It is about developing a personal sense of ownership among our team players, our volunteers.

Your volunteers are made up of a wide variety of talents and skills and even attitudes. They have shortcomings, strengths, and personal attributes. Your job is to bring these individuals together, working toward a common goal and then to motivate and inspire them to win. Winning occurs when the volunteer feels he or she is making a difference in the organization through their performance and helping the organization grow. We all have known great coaches, the kind that helped us stay focused, allowed us to believe more in ourselves, and enabled us to overcome disappointments. These great coaches harnessed our abilities and attitudes and somehow motivated us to worker harder than we even thought we could.

Our volunteers will not develop this sense of team, this feeling of commitment, unless they see the big picture. They must understand, and buy into, the purpose and meaning of their organization. It's a lot like having a team fired up to go into a big game, but unless they know that they have what it takes to win, and they see the reason to win, they will not complete their task and win the game. We call that desire to win commitment and to that we apply focus to stay on task, and use discipline to complete the task. Purpose and meaning are critical to the volunteer. Without a strong understanding of why our organization is doing something, the volunteer will not invest themselves. This investment must also strongly connect to their personal values.

Commitment to the organization must always follow this purpose or meaning. Volunteers do not give of themselves unless what they are doing has meaning. Volunteers want to see how what they are doing connects to a much larger, bigger picture. It sometimes seems that the task of the volunteer lacks importance. Our job, as coach, is to give that big picture to our players on a regular basis. Our players need to know how their task connects to build the dream. Ken Blanchard, in his book, *Everyone's A Coach*, co-authored with NFL great Don Shula, said that the essence of coaching is the attention to details and the monitoring of results. These, he says, are what help leaders realize visions and accomplish goals. It is this attention and monitoring that the volunteer coach does to help the volunteer stay on task and ensure that their work has meaning.

Realizing visions and accomplishing goals requires three core attributes from the volunteer coach: focus, empowerment, and praise. The coach must continually fine tune the volunteer's focus to insure that he/she grows in his/her volunteer intensity. The coach must let the volunteer know that he/she trusts him/her and have faith in his/her desire to get the work done, and lastly, the coach must simply never stop thanking the volunteers for work done well. Let's look at each of these three core attributes in more detail.

Focus requires that we insure that the volunteers all see the reasons, purposes and mission of the work they undertake. The organization's dreams must be in plain view, on the wall, on business cards, on the side of the vehicles. These dreams and goals must be always talked about and they must become clear so the volunteer is in clear focus about the reason for his/her work. The coach brings clarity to these goals and dreams. Without focus, there will be no commitment to these activities; people must see the purpose in their work. Volunteers make sacrifices to come to their organization and to continue to give. They must be clear about how their work contributes to the bigger picture.

Empowerment is the second core attribute of a successful volunteer coach. Volunteers need to feel an ownership of their tasks. If they are continually told what to do and never asked their opinions concerning the job, they will begin to act like many 9 to 5 employees. Those 9-5 employees are always waiting for a "Thank God it's Friday" day so that they can have some fun. Ownership of the workplace builds commitment in the hearts of volunteers. We, as volunteer coaches, must learn to trust the volunteers to get the job done. We must let them have enough rope to do the task their way and in their own style so long as the goals of the task are met and met on time. You can see that empowerment, then, requires both training and trust to work as a tool in the volunteer place.

Praise and appreciation for the volunteer and their work is the third core attribute. Volunteers, in fact all of us, work best when we feel that someone is aware of what we do and that they appreciate what we do. This praise for work done well must be continuous and in public view. Even when the volunteer may expect being thanked, it does go a long way toward building commitment. Patrick Townsend, in his book, *Recognition, Gratitude and Celebration*, gives us a few thoughts on the value of praise when he says, "Recognizing the achievement of others, expressing gratitude and celebrating success are all acts-and-responsibilities-of leadership." The role, then, of the coach, is to help the volunteer grow in knowledge and skill and then to, as Ken Blanchard says in *The One Minute Manager*, catch them doing something right. Praise does an important thing for volunteers, it reinforces the right activities. Think about it. As parents we praised our children when they did the things that we felt were correct behavior. And the children, desiring the treats or praise we gave them, repeated the good actions to gain more recognition. When we reward outstanding volunteer activity, we are letting them know that the organization appreciates their performance and that their activity is honored. It is a case where actions speak louder than words, particularly when the praise is given in public and with a gift of some kind saying thank you.

The final step in successfully coaching your team of volunteers is to insure that your players get the game plan. This game plan needs to be repeated everytime they get together, and information must flow in both directions. A coach shares all the information he/she has about the task underway. All players must have a chance to exchange information. John Maxwell, in his book, *Developing the Leaders Around You*, suggests that another important part of the communication process is huddling. He says that when a team huddles, it recalls the game plan and how it is to be implemented. These huddling sessions might include volunteer meetings, training sessions, or even impromptu coffee sessions between volunteers and the coaching staff.

28

SPECIAL EVENTS

We applaud each little success one after another...and the first thing you know, they actually become successful. We praise them to success!

Mary Kay Ash

Special events are a part of every volunteer organization's annual calendar. Many people are confused about why we do these type of events. They think special events are either to raise money or recognize volunteers. The truth is, they serve many functions. The key to all special events is that they should raise both money and friends for the organization. Alan Wendroff, in his book, *Special Events: Proven Strategies for Nonprofit Fund Raising*, makes an interesting statement about special events. He says, "Special events are the only fund raising program where potential givers come to your place, pay for the privilege of listening and learning what your agency is accomplishing."

A special event might be a volunteer recognition lunch or a black-tie dinner. It might be a 10 K run, a 5-mile walkathon, or an auction. All special events should be both fun-raisers and fundraisers. People attend special events to have fun and they are willing to spend money, if the cause is worthy. But, if the only reason you are holding a special event is to raise money, it may not be a good idea. There are better ways to fundraise than by holding a special event. Special events take a lot of volunteer time, cost agency budget and may cause a few people to buy tickets rather than support your annual fund. A special event is to raise friends, raise funds, and convey your message. An outstanding event does all three, not just one.

An event is special primarily because it serves special people. Your special people are your volunteers, community members, your board, and those community organizations that have supported you all year long. Events are also special because they raise money and friends for a very special cause. People will attend your activities because they believe in the mission of your organization. But remember that most community members that attend special events attend because of an exciting event, not because of the cause. People run in a 10K race because they like to participate in races, not because it's sponsored by the Elk Grove Unified School District.

Events of all kinds need to be run like a business. They need to be planned and then the plan must be followed. One important question in planning an event is to ask if you have strong enough leadership and a large enough core of volunteers. The event must also be consistent with your mission and it must appeal to your board members. Board members and volunteers must be brought in early in the planning process to develop buy-in from these folks. The event should have fun built-in for all partici-pants. The process of selecting the event is important because it involves groups of people meeting and gaining agreement about the value of the event.

One hidden motive for holding special events is to find potential volunteers, board members, and prospective donors. Success of a spe-cial event is a combination of increasing your volunteer base and lo-cating a strong donor base. Special events have many advantages to organizations; one is the potential to draw your paid staff and volunteers together, another is the confidence that your volunteer team feels as it accomplishes the tasks, and hopefully, the event gets people talking about your group.

You must be aware that special events are very labor-intensive. It takes longer and involves more volunteer help than you ever plan. Events tend to become more complex than they appear at first. Good planning and talking with others who have done a similar event is a good idea. Developing a budget will get you started as it forces you to think through the event. Budgeting will help you keep the expenses in line and let you think about that very important item called sponsorship.

Sponsorship is one of the keys to a successful event. Sponsors supply help to the organization, either donating services or dollars to your cause. You ask for support from sponsors that have a direct connection to your organization. Sponsorships improve the net income of special events and you should be specific about your needs. Remember that corporate sponsors expect to receive visibility from their involvement in your event. For them it is good business to invest in your event. They want people to recognize them as good citizens because they sponsor non-profit activities. Your task is to be very specific about your needs and ask for help where it is most needed.

Select board members and volunteers with a high degree of influence to serve as your leadership team. This team will invite other volunteers to take on various assignments. Use brainstorming as a technique to build a team spirit and to grow the feeling for the activity. Feeling an important part of the initial planning strengthens the volunteer's commitment. It becomes their event! The event needs a chairperson. This chairperson needs to have control of their time, be enthusiastic and have a wide circle of influence. It helps if they have strong organizational skills and if they are fun to be around. Your key volunteers will attract others who will pay to attend. It's always the person doing the asking that influences those being asked to attend. Having these volunteers on your committee helps build their commitment.

Before setting your dates, check with all of the agencies that sponsor similar events. Call the Junior League, the local visitors bureau, arts groups, churches, synagogues, even ask sports fans about upcoming activities that might interfere with your event. Give yourself enough time for planning. Leave a minimum of six months, or more lead time to get things underway. It takes this long to gather sponsorship dollars, a core of volunteers, and to select the best site to hold the event.

Think creatively about the location to hold your event. The three critical factors concerning the choice of site is location, cost, and size. Location must be appropriate to those attending, not too far away, and of interest to those planning to attend. One event my wife and I attended was sponsored by the University of Southern California as a wine tasting party. It was intended as both a fund raiser and a cultivation event. You paid money to attend (fund-raiser) and the event allowed those attending to be cultivated as a future donor. It was the location that led to a sell-out activity. The event was held at the old Western White House of Richard Nixon's presidency. The majority of the guests had never seen this location, and interest was extremely high to visit the home. One of the alumni of the university had purchased the home from the Nixon's and offered it as a site. Location, location, location it proved to be for this event.

Special events, when done well, have many advantages for your volunteer program. First, they allow a stage on which to recognize your outstanding volunteers, board members, potential donors and staff members. Second, it will be a showcase for your message to reach a new audience. This audience includes new friends attending the event, the media covering a community activity, and potential board members attending for the first time. And lastly, it will raise significant funds for your organization.

29

PRAISE!

The human spirit is nurtured by praise,
as much as a seedling is nurtured by the soil,
the water and the sun

Mario Fernandez

American corporations have long realized that thanking and recognizing employees improves morale and makes people feel good. As a volunteer leader walks around the volunteer place observing the volunteers working, they will observe good deeds and good actions. You should always watch for these special moments when a volunteer does something special for someone. At that moment of observation, you need to follow the spur-of-the-moment rule. It's similar to that well-known Nike advertising slogan, "Just do it." So at the moment of observing that special moment, go right on and praise that volunteer.

My friend and I were having lunch together and he was telling me about a special presentation made by one of his volunteers at a city council meeting the prior evening. He remarked about what a strong message that volunteer had made and what the impact will be for the agency. As we drove into the agency parking lot, my friend happened to see the volunteer's car and immediately stopped, got out of his car and took a business card out of his pocket. He turned the card over to the blank side and wrote a note to the volunteer, thanking him for that message before the council last night. He put that note of thank you under the volunteer's wipers on his car. I thought, what a wonderful, spur-of-the-moment way of recognizing this volunteer. If he had waited until the next volunteer meeting to recognize him, it would have lost some of the impact. In fact, even though my friend will say a few nice comments about the presentation at the next meeting, it's the spur-of-the-moment recognition that has the greatest impact.

I had a personal experience recently that reinforced this thinking. I had just driven out of my driveway heading to a meeting when I was thinking, "You know I really appreciate all the little things that my wife does for me." This thought, while nice, does not communicate the moment to my wife. If I had picked up my cellular phone and called her to say thank you, it would have been more effective by letting her know my feelings. So often, we have thoughts like this, but by the time we get to see the person again, the thought has drifted from our memory and another recognition moment has disappeared.

Saying thank you to volunteers is the best form of recognition. There needs to be many forms though of saying thank you. Sometimes it's face-to-face, following the catching of the volunteer doing something special. Sometimes, it's after the fact, in fact it might be because someone else brought the incident to your attention. It's important to realize that all forms of thank you are effective. We are sometimes misled into thinking that, unless we say thank you in person, or write a thank you note on a nice note card, it's not effective. I find that a thank you is a thank you, regardless of how you do it. I will use voice mail, often during a drive home from the office. Many times I will be stuck in traffic, thinking about a few things my volunteers had just completed. It might be that outstanding newsletter or that creative idea one volunteer made at the board meeting a few hours ago. I pick up the phone when I arrive home and leave a voice mail message for them, it will have the impact of making the volunteer know I do care and that I wanted to say thank you.

The computer brings us other high tech ways of saying thank you. E-mail is too cold for some folks to use as a forum for saying thank you, but I find it useful. I am a task-oriented person and I really do like receiving praise electronically. When someone e-mails me a note of thanks, it makes me feel good. In fact, I usually print it and put it on my refrigerator door under a magnet. I have also been known to tweet a volunteer a thank you. A tweet thank you has another possible advantage in that it might be a public thank you, as other people might receive it and see the praise. Putting the thank you on your facebook page will allow all the agencies friends to share the post.

One issue with recognition is that, as we continue to do it in only one form, it loses its impact. I can think about a group I worked with that had just completed its third volunteer recognition dinner. They had held the dinner at a very nice upscale hotel downtown, the same location for the past three years. I asked the group if they might be growing tired of the same location, and might they want to consider a new location next time? They said, almost in unison, "Yes, we are getting bored with this hotel banquet room". Good, I told them that I had located an unusual location, in fact it was a private home where we could roast a pig, have country music and even line dancing lessons! Everyone seemed excited at this prospect, but when I asked if they were ready to change, everyone said NO! I was shocked, and asked why they did not want to change, even though they had indicated boredom at our current setting, and that they showed interest with the new venue. They said the answer was tradition. I said carefully that they had only met at this hotel for three years. They said that's true, but it was a tradition to meet there.

Be careful; tradition will get your organization before you realize it. I am thinking about a group that has held a summer barbecue every summer for the past ten years. Nobody enjoys this event but nobody is willing to change or even to suggest a change. Why? You know the answer; it's a tradition for this group to hold a summer barbecue. Can you envision this group in ten more years? They are still holding this barbecue and nobody is attending. Silly? Yes. But accurate for many organizations. Can you think of a few organizations in your past that followed this same tradition even as attendance went down hill?

A suggestion to groups, particularly groups without established traditions, is to always change one of three things concerning recognition events. The three things are location, theme, and/or speaker. With every new event, either select a new and different location than past years, or alter the theme in a significant way, or at least change the speaker and topic. This will help to eliminate that tradition-building which locks groups in to the same old, same old problem.

The last thought about saying thank you is to do the thank you the right way. Let me tell you a short personal story to illustrate this point. Joan was working as a volunteer at an agency and enjoying her self. The director would walk from her office and when she spotted a volunteer would come right over to them and say, "Thank you for what you have done". At first, everyone thought that was a nice gesture, until they realized that she said the same thing to every volunteer. After hearing it for the seventh time one day, a group of them were enjoying a cup of coffee and one volunteer almost yelled, "She doesn't even know our names and she certainly doesn't know anything about our volunteer job!" He was right, this director had attended a seminar where the presenter told her to always thank volunteers for what they had done, and she took it to heart.

The problem is that all thank you's must be directed to a specific volunteer by name and the thank you must be for a specific task. She should have gone over to Joan and said, "Joan, I want to thank you for that outstanding newsletter that you wrote this month." Otherwise the thank yous are what I call throw-aways. Never waste the opportunity to thank a volunteer by making the thank you non-specific.

30

PUT AWAY YOUR TIN CUP!

You will find as you look back upon your life that the moments when
you have really lived are the moments when you have done things in
the spirit of love.

Henry Drummond

People help our organizations in two ways, by direct volunteering and
by donating services and products. When the annual awards dinner
comes around, we usually go out into the community and gather donations to be given out as recognition. We will visit local merchants and
ask for items to be given to the hard working volunteers in recognition
of their output. We usually don't look forward to these trips because
we feel as if we are begging our community businesses to help. I am
going to suggest that you put away your tin cup, stop thinking with a
begging attitude.

One day after Joan had called Jim, her local plumber, to clear the
drain in the restroom. Jim owned his own business and was well known
in the community. Jim came right over and did his normal magic, and

the drain was flowing once again. As he was putting away his tools, and Joan was writing out a check for sixty-five dollars, he said something that really opened her eyes. He asked why was she writing that check? Joan countered with the fact that the drains were now flowing and that was the charge. Jim suggested that he would like to make a donation of the service and asked if the money saved might be used to do more of the good work that he knows we do for the community. Wow! Did a light go on!

Jim was volunteering for the organization, but in a different way. He was volunteering as a service-in-kind volunteer. Jim was doing something very important, the same as our direct service volunteers; he was saving us budget dollars that we now had available to use for other needs. Joan thought, why not have another category of volunteer service, a service that allows local merchants to volunteer. That day she started calling this form of volunteering, Volunteer Vendors. Prior to this I always felt that I was begging local merchants for their support.

Volunteer Vendors are honest to goodness volunteers. They give of themselves and their business the same as your direct service volunteers give. Joan started talking to local merchants differently after this. She would approach a merchant by asking if they would like to volunteer. She started approaching the local business owners with this request. They would usually say that they had thought about volunteering, but that they had very little time as the business took most of their days. She explained that the organization had two ways to volunteer, direct service and vendor members. They expressed interest and she explained that her business people had an opportunity to volunteer by helping her with donations of service or products. They liked this approach because it made them a part of our program. It is important to think of this vendor member as a volunteer. Give them the same name badge as all your volunteers, include them in your list of volunteers, invite them to all volunteer functions. Always send your Volunteer Vendors invitations to all events and activities, and they will show up. You don't give free admission to most activities to your other volunteers and your volunteer vendors are no different. They will find that they do feel a part of your volunteer program and in fact, will thank you for allowing them to volunteer in their own unique way.

To make the volunteer vendor program work, it's important to follow three guidelines. First, don't go to the vendor member asking for something free every time you visit them. Remember that they are in business and that you normally used them for this service and paid for it. Save the donation for an important event where the help can be recognized, such as supplies or services for the annual recognition event. If one of your vendor members is the local printer in town, and they would design and print the programs for the black-tie awards dinner. Second, do not purchase products and services from another vendor and just visit your vendor member to get the free services and products. You can always find another business with a sale on something, but your vendor member deserves your support in return for the help they are giving. And third, when this vendor member gives you help, put it up in lights! At the event, make sure to announce the help you received from this volunteer from the stage and in the program. Have a special column in your newsletter that lists your vendor members. Also make sure that each newsletter features a vendor member, and their contributions, with a story about them and their business. Be sure to always feature them as Volunteer Vendors, not just businesses. Your Volunteer Vendors will receive the same benefits that all volunteers receive, they will feel good, meet interesting people and gain recognition at the events. They will also gain goodwill through their volunteering which will increase their business as well.

Volunteer Vendors come in a variety of forms. Almost everything you purchase can be found from a vendor member. Pro-bono services from attorneys, accountants, trainers, video producers, writers, to name a few, as well as printers, and repair services. If you think about it, if you have a volunteer vendor who volunteers doing accounting services for the agency, and another volunteer needs to find an accountant for their business, they might consider this volunteer. Of course; we do it all the time. You meet someone while volunteering, become friends, and make use of their talents for your business. It's called networking, and the more you publicize your Volunteer Vendors, the more it happens.

31

IS VOLUNTEERING DECLINING ?

Americans are volunteering less than they have in over a decade,
but why is unclear.

Danielle Kurtzleben | Staff Writer
U.S. News & World Report

A New Jersey newspaper reported that 3.6 million fewer people volunteered last year than had done so in 2006, when a record-level of Americans sought to fulfill their civic responsibility. It may be that the decline was that nonprofits failed to take full advantage of the volunteers who did step forward to offer their services.

Some people believe that it is the economy that is creating a shortfall of volunteer help. According to *Associations Now*, the United States saw its total number of volunteers drop to a 10-year low in 2013.

According to the latest data from the Bureau of Labor Statistics (BLS), the volunteer rate dropped 1.1 percent to 25.4 percent of the population in the year ending September 2013. They further tell us that "In a rather surprising twist given reports about how younger generations believe volunteer organizations and charities are the best way to improve society, volunteer rates were lowest among people aged 20 to 24 (18.5 percent), while people aged 35 to 44 were among the most likely to volunteer (30.6 percent)."

Nathan Dietz is senior research associate at the Center on Nonprofits & Philanthropy of The Urban Institute in Washington, D.C. It publishes *The Nonprofit Sector in Brief* and tracks giving and volunteering. Dietz recently joined the organization from CNCS and was there when the tracking started in 2002. Dietz said the 1.1 percent decline is the largest from 2006. He said the volunteering number for the past decade has been plus or minus 0.5 percent except when there was a large spike upward (27.4 percent to 28.8 percent) in 2003 and the big decrease (28.8 percent to 26.7 percent) in 2006.Certainly the 9/11 attacks created a large number of citizens wishing to help their communities. While you can blame the current economy for this declining membership, there appears to be many reasons for this loss. Let's discuss why this is happening, and what can be done to stop it. The economy is certainly an issue for many current and potential members. While there are many factors that contribute to this loss of volunteer hours, one of them is particularly worth noting – that of financial stress.

Verified Volunteers tells us that families throughout the country are struggling to make ends meet. "In single income homes, parents often struggle to earn enough with one income to support their entire family, an two-parent families don't always fare much better." *Newsweek's* recent article on the decline in volunteering identifies the pressing need for increased household earnings as a major contributor to the decline in volunteer hours. But there are other concerns that we need to address for this loss of membership growth.

In *Bowling Alone*, Robert Putnam makes a powerful argument that in the last several decades of the twentieth century, all sorts of community groups and in particular, service clubs have begun to fade. Putnam states that ..." It wasn't so much that old members dropped out, at least not anymore rapidly than age and the accidents of life had always. But community organizations were no longer continuously revitalized, as they had been in the past, by freshets of new members."

It is interesting to survey volunteering by demographic groups.

The following was compiled by the *Bureau of Labor Statistics* in 2015. The volunteer rate for men was little changed at 21.8 percent for the year ending in September 2015. The rate for women was 27.8 percent, down from 28.3 percent in the previous year. Across all age groups, educational levels, and other major demographic characteristics, women continued to volunteer at a higher rate than men.

By age, 35- to 44-year-olds and 45- to 54-year-olds were the most likely to volunteer (28.9 percent and 28.0 percent, respectively). Volunteer rates were lowest among 20- to 24-year-olds (18.4 percent). Teenagers (16- to 19-year-olds) continued to have a relatively high volunteer rate, at 26.4 percent. The volunteer rates for 35- to 44-year-olds and 55- to 64-year-olds declined.

Married persons volunteered at a higher rate in 2015 than those who had never married. In 2015, parents with children under age 18 were again more likely to volunteer than persons without children. The volunteer rate of persons without children under age 18 declined over the year, while the rate for parents with children under age 18 was little different from a year earlier.

Individuals with higher levels of education were more likely to volunteer than were those with less education. Among persons age 25 and over, 38.8 percent of college graduates with a bachelor's degree and higher volunteered, compared with 26.5 percent of persons with some college or an associate's degree, 15.6 percent of high school graduates, and 8.1 percent of those with less than a high school diploma. The rate of volunteering declined for persons across all levels of educational attainment in 2015.

Collecting, preparing, distributing, or serving food was the activity volunteers performed most often for their main organization in 2015. Other activities performed frequently were tutoring or teaching, fundraising, and engaging in general labor.

The *US News and World Report* stated, "While it might make intuitive sense that an improving job market would bring the rate down, that doesn't appear to be true. The volunteer rate hit its peak in the early 2000s, when the jobless rate was lower than it is now. In addition, as the Washington Examiner points out, "employed Americans tend to volunteer at higher rates than the unemployed or people not in the labor force."

Most volunteers were involved with either one or two organizations. In 2015, the main organization--the organization for which the volunteer worked the most hours during the year--was most frequently religious, followed by educational or youth service. Another 15 percent of volunteers performed activities mainly for social or community service organizations. Older volunteers were more likely to volunteer mainly for religious organizations than were younger volunteers. Of volunteers age 65 and over, 42.7 percent served mainly through or for a religious organization.

Three major issues confronting people as they consider volunteering are time, money and family. The volunteer feels that their time is impacted by both work needs and family responsibilities. These three issues usually come up during recruiting talks with potential volunteers. They will ask questions relating to how much time is expected of volunteers, and how can my family be involved in volunteer activities.

Time might be impacted by the age of the potential member and their place in the work world. For example, if the volunteer is older and already retired, then the time concerns are not as critical. But if the younger person is working longer hours or even working at more than one job, it will be a major concern. If the couple has small children needing lots of care and transportation, then time again becomes a major concern. As younger women move into volunteering, childcare usually takes a major role in the time arena. If both mom and dad are working, then childcare becomes an even stronger issue. It appears that time and the apparent lack of it in today's busy world of work and pleasure is a major issue. With the growth of single moms and dads childcare issues become even stronger. Time is an issue if the agency requires a weekly assignment for volunteers. There are options that agencies might consider in relationship to time concerns. They might allow work sessions less frequently than weekly and begin to use on-line meetings for training and orientation.

Money is an issue for many, even without considering the current economy. To many people in society volunteering has always been considered a rich person's game, even if that is a false perception. But still it does require money for both travel and meals as you volunteer. There is pressure in some agencies to contribute to the non-profit. While this is optional, it might still increase the pressure for those with limited incomes.

Family activities may require a majority of time and money for many younger members. Since the family requires so much more in the way of school and sports activities these days, it is a trade-off for many prospective volunteers. Many agencies are beginning to see that their members want to volunteer with their families. Many younger people want their children to get involved and get their experience volunteering with mom and dad. But it takes the agency planning ahead and taking on service projects that allow full family involvement. Young people want to build houses and playgrounds. They love the concept of *Habitat for Humanity* and the *Make A Wish* for families with children in a hospital.

32

WEB 2.0 AND VOLUNTEERING

"If your target audience isn't listening,
It's not their fault, it's yours"

Seth Godin, *Small is the New Big*

Web 2.0 is the term given to describe a second generation of the World Wide Web that is focused on the ability for people to collaborate and share information online. This indicates that Web 2.0 is a two-way exchange of information. While Boomers were using the Internet to view web pages, the younger folks were using the web to communicate with their peers. Their online experience was the beginning of Web 2.0, a totally new method of communications for the non-profit.

Seventy one percent of all adults are online. Most children are surfing the web today before they learn to ride a bike. Dr. Idit Harel says "technology is completely transparent to kids and they don't talk about technology, they talk about playing, building a web site, writing a friend about the rain forest." The technology is completely transparent to them.

Today most volunteers are texting and using social networks on a daily basis. Non-profits need to catch up with these new Web 2.0 tools. These are a number of social tools, not just the Internet. We live in a massively connected world with over one billion people connected to the Internet. More than 50 percent of US citizens have broadband access and these numbers increase daily..

We will rely a lot more on users generating and sharing content with each other. We are starting to see that everything we do online is going to have a social networking component. This social networking is an emerging phenomenon and will continue to develop in the years ahead. In Lynne Lancaster's 2010 book, *The M-factor*, she tells us that, "Many organizations do themselves a disservice by failing to let people know about the great work they do in making the world a better place." She says that we should make sure that our web sites, print materials, and even those volunteers emphasize our contributions to society.

People are ready to hear your stories and it can create valuable social capital with prospective volunteers as well as with the communities in which we do our volunteer work.

You might ask why social media matters. Just take a look at these numbers.

- 57% of all adults has a social media profile.
- 50% of all social networkers check their sites every day.
- Twitter use is growing at 400% per year.
- Facebook is the #2 destination on the web.
- The Average Facebook user has 120 friends.
- Over 850 million photos are updated to Facebook each month.

These are numbers that you can't ignore in your agency. It is time to develop a presence on Facebook, Twitter, LinkedIn, and YouTube. For young volunteers in particular, the most profound change is the pervasive connectedness of this new world. This is the constant connection to friends, and business peers. You need to learn to search, share, and interact in this new connected way. The key to attracting volunteers is getting the word out in a form that will interest them.

Social media can help your program in a few areas of marketing. First is building relationships with both volunteers and prospects looking to learn more about your program. Second is building the your agency brand, and maybe just as important is building your volunteer brand. Public image enhancement comes from any brand building and should be a primary focus of non-profits. Third it is a great method for building awareness of your upcoming social and fundraising events.

For over thirty years agencies have relied on the printed newsletter as the tool of connection and communication. But today a printed newsletter is only slightly higher on the value scale than junk mail. The problem is that few people have time to spend 20 minutes reading it and much of the information is not of interest to the reader. Enter Facebook and Twitter. Over 500 million people use Facebook and many agencies don't think it is relevant because they think their current members don't use it. The club that doesn't have an active website, and a Facebook Page or twitter account will most likely be the program that is consistently struggling to maintain volunteers. It's that simple.

Most of us are aware that online social networking is a big deal, but don't know what to do about it. A few of us use Facebook in our personal lives but aren't quite sure how it fits with volunteering. Social media includes a wide variety of Web tools such as websites, e-newsletters, Facebook, Twitter, Instagram, YouTube, and blogs. These social media tools are important because they keep the public and your volunteers informed about your activities.

Volunteer engagement is changing. What do you need to know about social media as a program manager? How can you use social media to promote volunteer opportunities and to recruit volunteers? Just how important is social media in your volunteer recruitment and retention plans. We know that Twitter, Facebook and YouTube pages, as well as blogs have successfully been used to draw attention to their organizations and volunteer opportunities. These tools can help you promote your volunteer opportunity on other social networking sites as well.

When thinking about ways to incorporate social media into volunteer recruitment and retention strategies, focus on engaging volunteers who are already in the social media space. These volunteers are more likely to engage actively on social media than those who are less comfortable or familiar with the technology. As volunteers leave their current positions, use this time to help them to evaluate positions for virtual Internet volunteering that are attractive to volunteers looking for short-term opportunities. Nearly a quarter of Internet users were willing to volunteer virtually, according to survey findings.

In an *AARP Study of the Implications for Volunteer Recruitment and Engagement* these four external organizations were using social media:

> *The American Red Cross* – The American Red Cross has virtual volunteers who scan and respond to conversations on social media in times of disaster.
> *The Alzheimer's Association* – The Alzheimer's Association utilizes Alzheimer's Ambassadors who incorporate social engagement in their advocacy efforts by, for example, reaching out to members of Congress on Twitter.
> *The United Way* – The United Way has a volunteer mobile application that allows users to geographically locate volunteer opportunities in their local areas.

Feeding America – Feeding America promotes small actions on their organization's social media pages to stimulate conversation and action regarding the issue of hunger in the United States.

If you do not understand social media and you have kids, just go down the hall and watch them for a while. If you don't have kids of your own, spend some time with a friend's kids. Watch them playing, communicating, and learning. Notice how much of their lives are being spent on line. Just visit an Apple store to watch the little ones play with technology.

According to Clara Shih in her book, *The Facebook Era*, "Thanks to their viral nature, we have reached the tipping point in the mass adoption of online social networks, and they will only continue growing in prominence and pervasiveness. According to Facebook, although it maintains an 85 percent or greater penetration among four-year U.S. universities, more than half of its users are out of college, and those 35 and older represent the fastest-growing demographic. This includes a majority of your volunteers.

Winogread in his book *Millennial Makeover*, tells us "younger are twice as likely as others to use the net, rather than the newspapers, to get information about political campaigns." The most recent US Presidential election demonstrated the use of social networking sites as a political recruiting tool. We can learn a great deal from Barack Obama's 2008 presidential campaign, which used Facebook and other social networking sites to rally millions of supporters and helped raise nearly $1 billion in grassroots campaign contributions. By the time Obama officially announced his candidacy six months later, it had already accumulated over 50,000 members and would eventually attract over 250,000 members.

Did you notice that I said attracted? That is exactly how social media works, it attracts. You do not recruit volunteers into your social media site, you attract them. In Tom Heads book, *It's Your World, So Change It,* he speaks of social media like online dating. He says, "You get on it to meet and interact with other people." You may hear about a website through Google, but you hear about social networking sites through friends. Your Facebook page gives everyone a sense of community where volunteers and friends find your updates concerning programs and events. Facebook gives you an area to promote events online, giving everyone the opportunity to receive invitations to specific events.

If the Xers and Millennial are the connected generation, then your agency needs to become the connected agency. According to the *Cone Study*, the bottom line is that the best way for organizations to reach young people with cause-related messages is to redefine the marketing experience. This study found that when a cause message is linked to a brand in an authentic and relevant way, it could gain the attention and respect of young people today.

Too many programs feel that once they put together a website, complete with an array of photos and maybe even a video clip or two that they are in the social media arena. Too many simply scanned their brochures and put them up on their web page, but this barely scratches the surface of what this change in the digital landscape is all about. For example a blog is not just another form of advertising your activities. *Blogger.com* says that a blog "is a personal diary, a daily pulpit, a collaborative space, a political soapbox, a breaking-news outlet, a collection of links, your own private thoughts, or memos to the world." They tell us that a blog is whatever you want it to be. There are millions of them, in all shapes and sizes, and there are no real rules. In simple terms, a blog is a web site, where you write stuff on an ongoing basis. New stuff shows up at the top, so your visitors can read what's new. Then they comment on it or link to it or email you.

This idea of personal interaction means it is not a corporate message, but it is opinions of individual volunteers being shared around the world. This is the beauty of the social networks as they are akin to public spaces where volunteers hang out. It is important to realize that while these Web

2.0 technologies are inexpensive compared to the older advertising methods such as buying space in a magazine or producing a television program, they will require time and learning. They are not magic! You will have to spend time and limited resources to make them work. But the connection you can gain with any of the social media tools is amazing. The value of a blog depends on the content you publish. The downside of a blog is that it takes effort to keep writing new entries and if you are not consistent it goes out of date fast. It's not as bad as a website that is out of date since the website tells the world about your programs and activities, while the blog covers opinions and thoughts of the writer. A blog is much less likely to date itself and will carry value for months, if not years. But like all social media, don't build any that you cannot maintain. It will frustrate many people but especially those younger people you are trying so hard to attract.

POSTSCRIPT

I have suggested in the Introduction that the purpose of this book was to help you build a more successful volunteer program, and that this is not a simple task. I also told you that I sense the paradigm changing from a control model to a model of collaboration. In closing this text, I would like to offer you my ten common-sense steps to building this professional volunteer program.

Step 1... We will stop looking for warm bodies.
We realize that all volunteers are professionals, people with skills and talents. We search for the work to be done at our volunteer places, and then find the right mix of people with the talent and available time to do the tasks. Warm bodies, we realize, are people with limited skills, being put into positions without much thought, and usually, on a temporary basis. Warm body recruiting is old thinking, stemming from the days when volunteers all did simple tasks of a common nature. People used advertisements placed on the shopping center walls to find these warm bodies and never considered marketing for specific talents and abilities. We want our volunteers to have skills, knowledge, positive attitudes, even passion and desire for their assignments.

Step 2... We realize that people really do not volunteer.
Our understanding is that people need to be attracted to volunteer. We are no longer willing to place flyers everywhere, and sit back waiting for the volunteers to arrive. The best recruiting happens when our volunteers ask their friends to volunteer with them. We conduct training for our volunteers in the best practices of asking. This may involve sales training, as we are aware that volunteers are fearful of asking one to volunteer. Their hesitation involves the fear of being turned down, or of feeling rejection. Our volunteers are given information on how to attract volunteers, why people want to volunteer, and what volunteers expect from volunteering.

Communication skills, including questioning, listening, and problem-solving techniques should be offered to volunteers to help them recruit others.

Step 3...We spend time finding out why our volunteers say "Yes".
We work to become close and intimate with our volunteers. We ask about their expectations and the variety of reasons that led them to our volunteer place. It is clear to us that if a volunteer says that they are lonely and they want to meet a few new people, that we have the task of introducing these volunteers to people. We understand that volunteers have expectations concerning volunteering and that if we don't exceed those expectations, the volunteer will lose interest. We know that the better we know our volunteers, the more connected the volunteers feel.

Step 4... We recognize people, not volunteers.
It is clear that when we recognize volunteers, that is, all volunteers in the same way and at the same time, we fail to recognize anyone. Each volunteer is a unique individual, and as such, needs to be thanked in a unique way. Some people do not wish to attend award programs, some will not show up for social activities, a few volunteers get embarrassed at being recognized in public. We must find ways to individually thank our volunteers for their work.

Step 5... We trust our intuition when we select new volunteers.
We understand that we work with lots of people and develop a strong sense of intuition. When a potential volunteer doesn't feel right to us, we say no. We don't accept volunteers when they show us those "red flags". Even though we check references and may even run criminal history backgrounds, it is really our "gut" feelings that determine our acceptance of new volunteers. At times, we are concerned about the new volunteers' attitudes. Sometimes it's the stated or unstated reasons that we hear or feel from our interview with the volunteer that causes us concern. We do not accept volunteers into our program if we have strong concerns because we are always protecting our clients and other volunteers.

Step 6... We have more than one way to volunteer in our place.

It is clear that many of our community members would like to be volunteers with us, but they cannot spare the time. Therefore, we have developed our volunteer vendor program allowing those individuals owning businesses to become volunteers and give us in-kind services. We realize that these volunteer vendors are truly volunteers and we treat them the same as our direct service volunteers. These volunteer vendors are invited to all functions, mailed newsletters, awarded recognition, and evaluated along with our direct service volunteers.

Step 7... We have a Boot Camp that all volunteers attend.

It is important that everyone working at our volunteer place be given complete orientation. This orientation serves as the boot camp for our new recruits. This includes both paid and unpaid staff. Our boot camp will include the history and mission of our organization, training in techniques and strategies for doing their assignments, and an understanding of the needs of our clients that we serve. We offer this boot camp at various times of day as well as weekends. Our program of orientation is conducted for large groups, small groups and, if needed, even one-on-one. We don't make volunteers wait months to attend boot camp, and we don't allow volunteers to perform assignments until they have completed the training.

Step 8... Everyone in our organization is a staff member.

It is clear to us that all our people are professionals, that they all have unique skills and talent. We could not function without this variety of people who work at our place. A few of these people are holding paid positions, and many of the people are volunteers. Both are important to our mission and to delivering the services to our clients. We call all these people staff members. We invite all staff members to meetings, allow everyone to use staff lounges, and we have staff recognition events. We understand that bringing all our staff together builds team spirit and helps people cooperate. Our staff recognize each other and understand each other's unique abilities and interests.

Step 9... We do not have a recruiting committee.

It's clear to us that the responsibility for recruiting new volunteers rests with all of our team players. The problem, we know, with a recruiting committee, is that the other staff members think that they should not be thinking about recruiting, that it is the responsibility of the recruiting committee. The reality of recruiting is that we should do it the Magic Way! Each volunteer is expected to find one new volunteer, and that volunteer they find should be as good as they are. We know that every volunteer has friends and that those friends are outstanding potential volunteers.

Step 10... We conduct Leadership 101 training on a regular basis.

Leadership 101 training helps those staff members who are ready to advance into leadership by giving them coaching, team building and communication skills. We also realize that when people are empowered to take charge, they build commitment to the organization. With all staff, being offered higher levels of responsibility, it builds their self-esteem and confidence. This leads to a stronger sense of teamwork and gives them a "we" rather than a "them" attitude. Leadership 101 needs to be offered on a regular basis and outside leaders should be brought in to continually enhance and freshen the training. This should be considered continuing education for your staff.

Conclusion...

These ten steps will allow us to move into this new paradigm. It will help us move from an organization that looked at numbers of volunteers to one that focuses on quality, service, and the customer. It will help us move from the thinking about paid staff vs. Volunteers, to being collaborative, respecting, honoring, and leveraging our diversity among all our staff.

"We wildly underestimate the power of the tiniest personal touch."

Tom Peters

ABOUT THE AUTHOR

Dr. Bill Wittich is a speaker and author in the field of nonprofit management. He travels an average of 100 days a year speaking to professional associations and non-profit agencies. His doctorate is from the University of Southern California and he has authored twelve books in the association and non-profit field.

He is a past President of the of the National Speakers Association Northern California chapter.

In 1990 Bill and his wife, Ann, launched Knowledge Transfer, a training and publishing organization based in Northern California.

Bill has been a member of Rotary International and is an instructor in their President Elect Training Seminar.

His background in non-profit, educational and governmental agencies allows him to bring day-to-day experiences into his writing and speaking.

The Wittich's enjoy living in Northern California where they enjoy cooking, collecting antiques, and learning about wine

To obtain additional information on training, or to schedule speaking engagements, please call 916-601-2485, email: billwittich@comcast.net or visit: billwittich.com